D0928065

BEFORE THE
RAINBOW FADES

BEFORE THE RAINBOW FADES

SUSAN GRANDES COHEN

PAINTINGS BY LUNDA HOYLE GILL

CRAWFORD HOUSE PRESS
BATHURST

I dedicate this book to my husband, Elisha, who welcomed me
into his culture, encouraged my efforts and lent unending support
to Lunda and me in this venture.
And to the memory of my aunt, Grace Mendelsohn Levy,
whose scholarly approach to all subjects inspired me to
pursue and attain, but who left this earth before the
completion of this manuscript. God rest her soul.

A CHP Production

Designed and published by
Crawford House Press Pty Ltd
PO Box 1484
Bathurst NSW 2795 Australia

Text copyright © 1994 Susan Grandes Cohen
Illustrations copyright © 1994 Lunda Hoyle Gill

ISBN   1 86333 098 4

All rights reserved. No part of this publication may be
reproduced, stored in a retrieval system, or transmitted
in any form or by means, electronic, mechanical,
photocopying, recording or otherwise, without the
prior permission of the publishers.

Printed in Hong Kong

10 9 8 7 6 5 4 3 2 1

CONTENTS

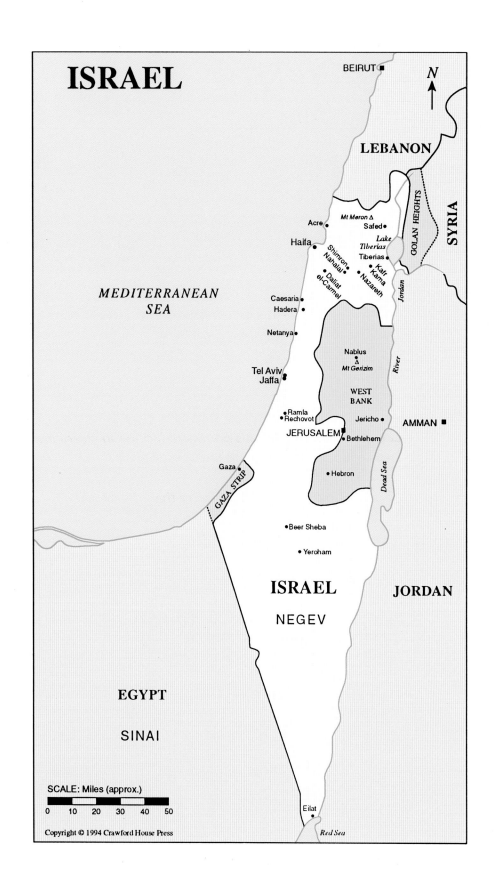

ISRAEL

N

BEIRUT

LEBANON

GOLAN HEIGHTS

SYRIA

Acre

Mt Meron △
Safed

Haifa

Lake Tiberias

Tiberias

Shimron
Nahalal

Kafr
Kama
Nazareth

Daliat
el-Carmel

MEDITERRANEAN SEA

Caesaria

Hadera

Netanya

Nablus
△
Mt Gerizim

Jordan

River

Tel Aviv
Jaffa

WEST
BANK

Ramla
Rechovot

Jericho

AMMAN

JERUSALEM
Bethlehem

Gaza

Dead Sea

Hebron

GAZA STRIP

Beer Sheba

Yeroham

ISRAEL

JORDAN

NEGEV

EGYPT

SINAI

SCALE: Miles (approx.)

0   10   20   30   40   50

Copyright © 1994 Crawford House Press

Eilat

Red Sea

vi

A NATIVE AMERICAN PRAYER

Anonymous

O' Great Spirit
whose voice I hear in the winds,
and whose breath gives life to all the world, hear me!
I am small and weak, I need your strength and wisdom.

Let Me Walk In Beauty, and make my eyes ever behold the red and purple
sunset.

Make My Hands respect the things you have made
and my ears sharp to hear your voice.

Make Me Wise so that I may understand the things you
have taught my people.

Let Me Learn the lessons you have hidden in every leaf
and rock.

I Seek Strength, not to be greater than my brother,
but to fight my greatest enemy – myself.

Make Me Always Ready to come to you with clean hands
and straight eyes.

So When Life Fades, as the fading rainbow, my spirit
may come to you without shame.

FOREWORD

I am happy to have the opportunity to write a foreword to this book which so faithfully presents the beautiful and unique aspects of Israel.

It was a splendid idea to publish a volume based on the research of Susan Grandes Cohen and strikingly illustrated with attractive portraits by Lunda Hoyle Gill. The singular and most interesting mosaic of Israel's population comes to life on these pages.

Israel is a melting pot of Jews from all over the world and a haven for people of different religions. From antiquity to the present, groups from varied backgrounds have lived together in this region. Their coexistence benefits the country and the entire area, and enriches the cultural fabric of Israel.

From the descriptions and attitudes of the individuals depicted in this positive and lovely book, it is clear that they all desire peace. Only a true and lasting peace will bring us the tranquility and security which our pioneering ancestors longed for when they came to our country.

I congratulate all those responsible for the publication of this volume and hope that its readers will respond to its message of peace and coexistence among all those living here, whatever their origin.

Reuma Weizman
Wife of the President of Israel
Jerusalem, February 22, 1994

ACKNOWLEDGMENTS

This book was the result of a tremendous team effort. I wish to express my gratitude to everyone who, even in the smallest way, participated in helping me write this book.

My love and admiration to the original team of Lunda Hoyle Gill and Elisha Cohen, our translator, guide, driver, paint squeezer and security blanket.

To Dantchu Arnon, a photographic journalist whose professional photos in the "Diary" chapter – my heartfelt thanks for that and all the extra work he so willingly performed. I must also thank Dantchu's wife Nomi, who often and always enthusiastically joined our group on some of our ventures. To my wonderful friend with broad shoulders, Essia Steinfeld, thanks sweetheart!

To Ruth Dayan, a dear and treasured friend who introduced us to some of the subjects that appear in this edition and who tirelessly answered my probing questions.

To Sefi Hanegbi, who acted as our guide, translator and storyteller about the desert Bedouin – my gratitude.

And to all my family and friends, too numerous to mention, without whom a word could not be written – many, many thanks.

Finally, to my dear friend and mentor, John Bradford, for reading, re-reading and re-reading my manuscript through to its final form – my deepest appreciation.

The catalyst for the book – a sole pair of leather shoes surrounded by the influence of Western culture, the Adidas, the Nikes, and so on.

INTRODUCTION

I consider this book an anthropological romance. The romance began with a great love of the land of Israel and of all the people who inhabit her, whether Jew, Christian or Moslem. Over the years, they have welcomed me into their homes and openly shared their cultures. If there exists any question of the possibility of peaceful coexistence between these groups, this work should erase any shadow of a doubt.

The story is anthropological in the sense that it addresses the destinies of people caught up in a sometimes painful cultural transition. My purpose in writing this book was as much a scholarly pursuit as an attempt to capture the vanishing cultures of Israel through my pen and the eyes and oils of Lunda Hoyle Gill, the distinguished ethnographic artist whose powerful portraits illuminate the text so beautifully. My purpose was not to write a political treatise. Although fully aware of the political situation while I write, and its tragic ramifications for all of these people, I have purposefully skirted the political issues to give you, the reader, a chance to know and love these people as I do.

If this collaboration serves as a tiny time capsule to help future historians better understand the land of Israel and its colorful peoples, I will have accomplished my purpose. With that goal in mind, I determined from the start to abstain from anything of a political nature. Instead, you will find this book to be about individual members of ten cultures, a small representation of the more than 100 cultures living in a comparatively tiny area of some 8,000 square miles, a little bigger than the State of New Jersey. As you can see from the map, Israel's neighbors are Egypt, Jordan, Syria, Lebanon and the Mediterranean Sea. The main languages spoken there are Hebrew, Arabic and English, and the three major religions are Judaism, Islam and Christianity.

I have been visiting Israel periodically since 1960. Through the years, I have heard how the first generation of immigrants flocked to her shores, ploughed the rocky earth and, against all odds, fashioned a flourishing agrarian nation. The greening of Israel was accomplished by the collective sweat and zealous cooperation of divergent peoples working toward a common goal. Then sadly I have watched successive generations of Israelites transform their land, once appealing in both its simplicity, charm and open-armed acceptance of diverse and beautiful cultures, into high-density concrete bastions resembling New York, Los Angeles or any other Western megalopolis. Unfortunately, what took America 200 years to do, Israel and her neighbors are trying to do in little more than forty-five years.

The concept of space has been lost in the rush toward economic development. The once-expansive and beautiful shores of the Mediterranean, where I used to walk and enjoy the sun, sea and fresh air, have been obliterated by high-rise hotels, the new sentinels of the coast. The generation of pre-1948 Palestinians, which was imbued with the idea of building a homeland free of persecution and consumed with survival, has been superseded by its post-industrial progeny. The kibbutzniks have given way to the "yupniks" whose goals and ideals are the acquisition of MBA degrees, BMW automobiles, fax machines, computers and other technological badges of success. But, in their defense they, as well as any other nation, have every right and should make every effort, to enter the 21st century, on an equal footing with everyone else. Unfortunately, in their pursuit of fortune and social position, the Mediterranean people have yet to learn what the Western nations regret, but can no longer control.

The amalgamation of the peoples of Israel has become most distinct in the latter part of the 20th century through intermarriage and adaptation of Western culture. What remains are the senior members of each community frantically trying to hold onto the few vestiges left of their origins. I do not stand in judgement of any of these groups, nor do I refute or support any claims made by my interviewees or any representatives.

To students of history of all ages, professionals and amateurs, I apologize for the brevity of some of my historical descriptions. Often, reliable information was simply not available, although each group represented here has a long and fascinating past. When references are made to the Diaspora, it is important for the reader to understand that it refers to all Jewish people not living in the land of Israel. Although I speak about Arabs and Jews, it is equally important for the reader to know that both groups are part of the Semitic race. The Arab populations are made up of Moslems and Christians. Jews are followers of a religion, although very often they are referred to as a race of people.

Many writers have used the phrase "mosaic" culture of Israel, but I must question for how long? As a whole, the inhabitants of the country, no matter what their religious belief or affiliation, enjoy the benefits of that country. They are landowners, businessmen, emissaries of God and professionals.

The title of the book came as an inspiration resulting from one of my trips. I was visiting a kibbutz (a collective farm). Outside the children's house was a table where the sand-playing children had left their shoes. A sole pair of brown leather hi-tops were reminiscent of the immigrant children's shoes when they arrived on the shores of America. But surrounding this single pair of shoes was the material culture of the Western world, the Nikes, the Adidas, and so on. It is what remains.

Addendum: September 1993

What excitement! At this time the Israelis and Palestinians are on the verge of signing peace agreements as are Jordan and Syria. I believe in the process of peaceful coexistence as I have shown you in my book.

If all sides drop their weapons and raise their hands in unity and mutual cooperation, they will be assuring a lasting peace for their children and for all the generations that follow. Let us all pray that we have finally turned a page in Middle East history – the *final* page.

A BUKHARAN DANCER

Bracha Eliezerov was born in Bukhara in 1913. Bukhara lies in the Khanate region of Soviet Central Asia, now known as Uzbekistan. Uzbekistan consists of five regions or republics, each of which shares at least one border with Iran, Afghanistan or China. Since it was positioned along an ancient trade route which linked Turkey and China, Bukhara's textile industry flourished between the 15th and 20th centuries. Via camel and mule caravans, they traded locally produced fabrics for China's silk, spices, gold and salt.

Despite the invasions of Alexander the Great and Genghis Khan, both of whom wreaked havoc upon the area, Bukhara survived, probably because, as evidenced in the last Soviet invasion of Afghanistan, the rugged terrain and harsh climate made this land untenable to the invaders. In retrospect, it is easy to see why these hostile incursions were foredoomed. From its highest peak to its lowest valley, Uzbekistan's elevations range from 24,590 feet to 433 feet below sea level. The incredible extremes of climate, the stretched supply lines and the unexpected ferocity of the defending Uzbek tribesmen proved to be unconquerable.

Except for a very few ultrarich industrialists, the Central Asians have lived in comparative squalor throughout history. And, especially after the late 1500s, when Ivan the Terrible was in power, the Khanate region became a center for Islam, and the Jewish minority was targeted for persecution. The Diaspora (the dispersion of Jews to areas outside Palestine) began in 597 BCE, nine years after Nebuchadnezzar overran Jerusalem, razed its temple and carried large numbers of captives to Babylon. Later, Nebuchadnezzar deported all the Jews of the Northern Kingdom of Israel. Most of these Jews settled in the Caucasus (that range of mountains between Europe and Asia, extending from the Black Sea to the Caspian Sea). For the most part, the Jewish expatriates were treated well. In Babylon, this period of captivity has proven to be an extremely creative era in Israel's religious life and literature. During the Exile, as it is now referred to, the oracles of Ezekiel and Second Isaiah were composed, the Deuteronomy was edited and brought up to date and the "Priestly" edition of the Pentateuch was written.

Until 988 CE, when Vladimir I converted Russia to Christianity by fiat or sanction, Russian Jews lived in comparative harmony with non-Jews. They were tolerated socially if not totally integrated. But after the compulsory conversion edict, the Jews were treated as unwelcome foreigners, isolated, ostracized and derided as subhuman. They were tolerated only as moneylenders, musicians and entertainers. But they were heavily taxed, forbidden to own property and forced to close down their shops and businesses. Yet, the Russian Jews survived and some, whose talents were unique and essential to the economy, even prospered.

In 1530, Ivan the Terrible decreed that all Jews who refused to embrace Christianity be banished from Russia. Many of those who left settled in Poland. Those who remained and defied Ivan's edict were sentenced to death by drowning. Many Jews went through the motions of converting, but continued to observe the Jewish faith in secret.

The Time of Troubles was the appellation given to the years 1604 to 1613. Russia was torn by civil war, invasion and political confusion. The landed gentry (boyars) struggled for supremacy against the fierce Cossacks, who led the insurgent lower classes. The Poles and Swedes took advantage of the distracted Russians and met little opposition when they invaded Western Russia. In this era of anarchy, the non-aligned Jews (even those posing as Christians) were terrorized by both warring factions, and their homes were pillaged by the ill-equipped Cossacks. Many moneylenders were slain by impoverished debtors, who were exhorted by their desperate leaders to blame all their troubles on the despised Jews.

A semblance of order was restored in 1611, when a consortium of boyars formed a national militia which drove the Poles out of the northern and eastern provinces.

In 1613, the Land Council (a national assembly) crowned Mikhail Romanov Czar. This not only began a firmer establishment of serfdom; it resulted in the abolishment of local self-government.

Under Czarist rulers, the so-called "Jewish Problem" resulted in the harshest, most systematic "solutions": assimilation by conversion; expulsion; or subjection to "social engineering," whereby Jews were dehumanized to a state of semislavery and assigned to compulsory work projects. When one remembers the pyramid-building Jewish slaves of ancient Egypt, here was a bitter example of history repeating itself.

Declared "undesirable aliens", the Jews were confined to a Pale of Settlement, which consisted of twenty-five western provinces between the Baltic and Black seas.

Forbidden to travel or live beyond the Pale, work at anything but "productive labor" on the harsh land, attend Jewish schools or wear traditional garb,

Jews were subjected to periodic "Jew hunts", pogroms and unrelenting humiliation at home and in the workplace. Although many Jews were conscripted into military service, they were denied advancement in grade and banned from all military schools and institutions of higher learning.

Perhaps the most significant date in Russian Jewish history was 1881. In that year of infamy, Russia became the only country in Europe where anti-Semitism was declared the official policy of the state. This began a massive exodus of Jews from Russia. By 1906, several million Jews had either emigrated or been expelled, most of them going to the United States. Those Jews remaining in Russia were subjected to increased savagery, and escape to Palestine became the "impossible dream" that burned in the hearts of all Russian Jews, be they Zionist, Orthodox or secular. You may wonder why all the Jews did not leave under such severe conditions. Those who could did. The people who had no means, those who were physically incapable and those who had nowhere to go remained.

The tyrannical Romanov Dynasty reigned for 300 years, but tottered in 1914 when Russia went to war with Germany over the control of the Balkans. Without the enthusiastic support of the army, and with the return of the outlawed Bolshevik leaders, Lenin and Trotsky, the malcontents (secretly abetted by the Germans) revolted against the Czarist regime. The government troops who were sent to quell the uprising joined the insurgents instead, and by September, 1917, the Bolsheviks had seized control of the government. Weary of the casualties, the lack of food and coal and the insensitivity of the Czar, the Russians withdrew from the war. The Bolsheviks (soon to be renamed the Russian Communist Party) moved the Russian capital back to Moscow from Kiev, adopted a red flag and organized the Red Army under the leadership of Leon Trotsky. The considerable number of anticommunists organized the White Army, and the battlelines were drawn. The peasants, fearing they would lose their lands if the Reds lost, supported them. The Whites, with the support of troops from France, Japan, Great Britain, the USA, and other countries opposed to Communism, found their ill-assorted allies to be fearful of engaging in another war so soon after World War I, and, therefore, were woefully reluctant to fight the highly motivated Red Army. The Red Army won this battle, but soon was confronted with a succession of brushfire wars on several fronts, including Vladivostok, where the Japanese invaded Siberia on December 30, 1917, and where an army of Czechs (former Austrian prisoners of war) had already begun to march toward the same city, hoping to join Allied forces in Europe.

By 1921, Russia was exhausted after seven years of World War I, revolutions, civil war and invasions. The civil war alone claimed the lives of 20 million Russians from starvation, fighting and epidemics. So, after the bloody mutiny and uprising of the sailors at Kronstadt, the situation finally forced the Communist Party to elect Lenin General Secretary and adopt the Lenin-sponsored New Economic Policy (often referred to as the NEP), which drastically changed many of the government's stringent economic policies. Farmers no longer were required to give most of their product to the government. Instead, after paying taxes, they were allowed to sell freely in the open market. Small industries and retailers now could operate autonomously, but the government retained control of banking, transportation, heavy industry and foreign trade. The economy began slowly to recover under the NEP, but Lenin's hardline detractors in the Politburo protested that the NEP was too Western and non-socialist in concept.

The United Soviet Socialist Republics (USSR) was established in 1922, linking Russia and Transcaucasia into one federation. Shortly thereafter, Tadzhikistan, Turkmenistan and Uzbekistan joined the USSR.

Since much of the Russian Revolution and the subsequent civil war raged across the Jewish Pale of Settlement, and because Lenin and Trotsky were Jews, the White antirevolutionary forces mistakenly assumed that the traditionally anti-war Jewish masses were behind the Revolution. Venting their wrath on the people of the Pale, the White armies slaughtered more than 100,000 Jews.

Under Lenin, anti-Semitism was considered a punishable crime against the Soviet Union, and universities and professions were opened to the Jews.

In 1922, Lenin became seriously ill and withdrew from office. The resultant struggle for power in the Politburo was decided by the election of Joseph Stalin as Lenin's successor. Trotsky and several other Leninists were forced to flee for their lives. Lenin died in 1924, and the NEP died with him. Stalin gradually rid himself of all his political adversaries and, by 1928, assumed the role of total dictator. His first Five-Year Plan reversed all the gains attributable to the NEP, and the peasant farms were combined into government-controlled collectives. As a result, the farmer was reduced to the ignominy of serfdom. To show their resentment, many farmers burned their crops and destroyed large numbers of their livestock. This so infuriated Stalin that he summarily sent millions of dissident peasant families to prison labor camps in Siberia and Soviet Central Asia. The dictator further disillusioned his constituents by forcing millions of able-bodied men, women and children into hard labor in government factories. In a mad rush to dramatically expand the production of heavy-industry products, such as chemicals, construction materials, machine tools and steel, Stalin manifested a callous disregard for the Soviet workers' health, safety and welfare.

In 1933, Stalin tightened his choke hold on the country by instituting the Great Purge, which resulted in the expulsion of 1 million members of the Communist Party. There ensued a reign of terror, with Stalin in complete control of everything and everyone in the USSR. With his secret police (the dreaded NKVD) arresting thousands of citizens whom they suspected of disloyalty, rigged trials and forced confessions of "crimes against the nation", untold numbers (some say millions) were either shot or sent to labor camps. With Stalin controlling the news media and everything published, taught or spoken in public, the citizenry and the outside world had no way of knowing the full extent of Stalin's atrocities against the Soviet people.

Along with the abolition of most Leninist doctrines, all so-called civil rights were revoked, including the law against anti-Semitic behavior. Predictably, as always happens in times of economic stress, the hapless Jews were targeted as the cause and, therefore, the enemy.

Perhaps now you can empathize with the plight of Bracha Eliezerov and her family. Not only were they living under the despotic rule of the power-crazed Stalin, but they were subjected to increasingly anti-Jewish denigration by the Moslem government of Uzbekistan. Besides being more heavily taxed than their Moslem neighbors, Uzbek Jews were forced to wear demeaning identification symbols and were constrained from working at all but the most menial labor.

Why this oft-repeated persecution of the Jews? It cannot be because Jews "look different", since their color and facial characteristics are no different from those of many other ethnic groups.

The best answer seems to lie in the historical fact that Jews have traditionally been "people of the book". Their very exclusion from social interaction with their non-Jewish neighbors, their coping with "apartness", has brought about an awareness of the importance of education and advancement. It may also have served as a solace to these people, an opportunity to escape into a book from the harsh realities of life. Wherever not forbidden free access to opportunity, many have risen to high positions in banking, industry and the arts. This is precisely what happened in Germany before World War II. The economy was collapsing; Jews held high positions and many prospered; Hitler rose to power by promising the hungry people a stronger economy by solving "the Jewish Problem", and the rest is history.

Eli Weisel, in his book *Jews of Silence* depicts the plight of Soviet Jews through their searing and suspecting eyes. After generations of persecution, sublimation and suppression, it is understandable that a Bukharan Jew views strangers with a measure of mistrust. This attitude extends even to other Jews. Thus, I was not surprised when I met Bracha Eliezerov to find her attitude somewhat timorous. Elisha, Lunda and I, each laden with equipment of all sorts such as a video camera, photographic cameras, easels, canvases, paints, a recording device and notebooks, waited rather uncomfortably in the hallway while Bracha unlocked the entrance door. I made it a point to note the number of locks on the door as it took so long. There were five! It was very surprising to me in a country that holds their elderly in great respect and crime in general is very low. We arrived at Bracha's Tel Aviv apartment at the appointed time. Bracha, who lives alone, finally admitted us, and although she was not exactly ungracious, she began the encounter with complaints of backache and general malaise. Obviously, she was uncomfortable in the presence of these three people who, for reasons she only half understood, wished to paint her portrait and interview her. The window of her living room was opened for air and light, and through that opening poured a deluge of cacophonous city sounds: pregnant buses trundling and beeping through the narrow street below; car horns honking angrily; bicycle bells ringing; street vendors hawking; and dogs barking. It was an unnerving background for an interview, I thought. But Bracha seemed not to notice it. Nor did Lunda, who locked in on her subject, blocking out everything except the task at hand. This was the first time I had watched Lunda at work, I realized, and both Bracha and I were fascinated by the calm, swift way she positioned her subject in a chair, sat on a chair opposite her subject and, propped on another chair, positioned her canvas. She squeezed her paints on her palette and started painting with deft, sure brush strokes. No rough pencil sketching, no hesitation. She was so awesome to watch, I had to remind myself that I was there to interview my first subject, not to watch Lunda at work.

After several desperate but vain efforts to shut out the noise without shutting out Lunda's light, I turned on my video camera and began to record my conversation with Bracha. We spoke in Hebrew, and, as her story unfolded, I came to realize that her tiny, L-shaped sitting room was actually a mini-museum of her earlier, bittersweet memories. Against one wall stood an ornate wooden sideboard, with spiral legs supporting drawers and cupboards. The center of this wall featured a television set, above which was hung a glass-enclosed curio cabinet. On the glass shelves were her collection of souvenirs of places in Europe she had visited. These were intermingled with similar mementos sent to her by her three children, whose musical careers necessitated a great deal of traveling. On the wall surrounding this cabinet were hung all manner of memorabilia: hand-tinted photographs, the type of photo coloring practised before Kodachrome or Ektachrome were introduced, with exaggerated colors, depicted Bracha and her late husband in their youth. Another tinted photo of them in native costume, fading from years of exposure to sunlight, proves now to have been an ironic illustration of this book's title. Randomly juxtaposed on shelves were vases of artificial flowers, a few plaques awarded to the Eliezerovs for cultural contributions, a modern photo of a grand-daughter, ornately hand-painted Bukharan platters and a framed, embroidered Jewish blessing. Pushed against the opposing wall was a dining table. It was covered with a crocheted cloth, waiting patiently for the time company would come. Above the table hung a large photograph of Bracha, her husband and children, all in native garb, enjoying some festive occasion with a once-famous Israeli actor. Draped over the edge of the frame was a faded red ribbon, with a single fossilized rose dangling from its middle. The young Bracha in the photo was quite beautiful, and when she spoke to me about that evening and who everyone was, her eyes glistened wistfully. This was Bracha's world.

During a lull in our conversation, I noticed that Bracha seemed ill at ease. Perhaps, after looking at the photographs of herself as the beautiful young dancer she once was, she was made aware of the cruel lines that years of suffering had etched in her face. I could see that she was becoming concerned about how Lunda was portraying her. I had noticed a radio-cassette player on a shelf, with a few audio cassettes beside it. To lighten the mood, I asked Bracha if she had any music from Bukhara. Her eyes lit up as she happily popped a cassette into the tape deck, and when the rhythmical beat of the music filled the room, Bracha became a woman transformed. Even in her chair, she could not sit still. Her arms moved gracefully through the air, her body straightened proudly and her spirit seemed to leap back in time to days that used to be. Gone were the back pains and the distrust as she rushed to her bedroom to bring out her lovely Bukharan costumes, dancing boots and intricately woven headgear. She tirelessly tried on all of her wardrobe for Lunda, dancing all the while. She was delightful to watch, and her worn costumes were still magnificent. Lunda clicked away with her camera, for the intricate detail that would follow in the finished painting, and I videotaped her delightful performance. When Lunda decided which costume she wanted Bracha to wear for the portrait, we actually had to ask her to turn off the music so she would sit quietly. She again became the elderly woman, but she sat more erect, less lethargically now as Lunda resumed her painting. The music and the dancing had been exhilarating for all of us, and I think it sustained Bracha for the balance of our interview. It certainly made Lunda's work easier, and I cannot help believing that, but for the music, Bracha would have been less willing to tell me the painful story of her escape from Bukhara.

This is Bracha's story.

Having been born to a mother who was a professional dancer and a father who was an accomplished musician, it seemed preordained that Bracha would follow in her mother's footsteps. Not only did she become a featured dancer, but she married a musician, one of the three brothers Eliezerov, whom she met while performing in a Bukharan nightclub.

Because the city was a key stopover point for traders *en route* to and from China, Russia and much of Europe, its nightclub business flourished. The Eliezerov brothers performed long hours nightly, earning a considerable amount of money. Bracha, who retired from dancing to give birth to their first child, a daughter, remembers this as the happiest time of her life, even though anti-Jewish discrimination was on the increase. Realizing the situation could only worsen, it was again every Jew's renewed dream to leave Bukhara and emigrate to Palestine. However, since travel documents were denied them, the only possibility of leaving Bukhara was by escaping. As alluded to earlier, the nearly impassable terrain and the punishing extremes of weather in this region discouraged all but the young, the hardy or the desperate from attempting to scale the intimidating mountains or cross the barren desert. Many of those who dared to try escaping perished from starvation. Others, out of sheer exhaustion, gave up the attempt, returned to Bukhara and were imprisoned.

It was in 1933, with the real threat of a German invasion, that rumors of a plot to kill any Bukharan Jews who had accumulated money circulated throughout the Jewish community. On the eve of the intended executions, the Eliezerov brothers fled on foot and crossed the Amu Darya River into Afghanistan. Twenty-year-old Bracha remained behind with her infant daughter. To support herself and her child, she resumed her dancing career and eked out a modest living for two years. Meanwhile, having heard that the Eliezerov brothers had made good their escape, and feeling that her daughter was now old enough for the arduous trek, she joined a group of Jews who were planning to escape from Russia along the same route taken by her husband. Unfortunately, the escapees were apprehended by the Soviet authorities at the Afghan border. The captured men were sent to prison; the women and children were returned to Bukhara. With a heavy heart, Bracha once more resumed her dancing. She wondered if she would ever see her husband again or see the Holy Land. When she learned from the Jewish community that another escape group was forming, she unhesitatingly contacted them and signed on. This time, she was assured, the route would be safer, through Tehran. It should be remembered that at this point in history, there were no such things as passports, only travel documents. Bracha and the other members of this group left without any papers, making the intended journey even more jeopardized. Taking very few supplies, to avoid the suspicious eyes of the Soviet authorities, they took a train to the town of Ashkhabad, near the Iranian border. From here, after deciding against shopping for supplies and possibly revealing their intentions to the ever-watchful border guards, the desperate adventurers set off on an uncharted climb of the Elburz Mountains, never knowing when they would drink the next cup of water or eat the next crust of bread. After seven interminable days and nights of arduous climbing without sustenance, Bracha's two-and-half-year-old daughter died in her arms. Other youngsters died from thirst and starvation and were buried where they died, in unmarked graves.

Dazed, despondent and consumed with guilt for having contributed to the death of her firstborn, Bracha had no choice but to stagger along with her despairing companions. The single thought that sustained her was that, having already paid a mother's ultimate price, she must reach Palestine or die in the attempt.

Ironically, only two days later, on the eve of Passover (a Jewish holiday celebrating the Jewish exodus from Egypt with Moses), the group stumbled

13

upon the village of Kaakhka, which straddles the border between Iran and the former Soviet Union. They were taken in by other Jews living there and remained for one month, gradually recuperating sufficiently from their punishing trek to push onward. Camels and a guide were provided by their Kaakhka friends to take them the short but rugged distance to Meshed, Iran. From this point, they traveled by bus for three days to the city of Tehran.

Buoyed momentarily by the realization that only approximately 1,000 miles separated her from her husband, Bracha and her friends applied for the required Iranian papers which would allow them to cross the borders into Palestine. To their dismay, their requests were denied.

Fortunately, Bracha was able to make contact with her husband, who had managed to reach Palestine in 1935. But it took him two more years of pounding on official doors before he was able to obtain a certificate of immigration for Bracha and send it to her. Since, as I have told you, there were no passports or visas during this time. The official doors that Bracha's husband was pounding on were those of the representatives of the British government ruling Palestine. The coveted document he was trying to obtain was actually called a certificate of immigration, issued specifically for emigration to Palestine. During World War II, the Joint Jewish Committee was working on getting the British Minister of External Affairs to issue these documents. Finally, after a great deal of spent energy by this committee, 100,000 certificates of immigration were issued in the 1930s. Bracha, with the help and persistence of her husband, was among the lucky recipients. But prior to her obtaining this document Bracha endured a tremendous period of frustration. She worked at many menial jobs and only occasionally performed as a dancer. But, as a displaced Bukharan Jew in a predominantly Moslem country, it was extremely difficult to find more remunerative employment.

Finally, in January, 1937, Bracha cleared the myriad paperwork hurdles. The waiting was over, but the trek to Palestine was to prove to be almost as difficult as the journey from Bukhara to Tehran. Even with the travel document in hand, Bracha had to walk through hostile territories, Moslem-ruled countries. The route she took was from Tehran, through Damascus, Syria, into Palestine. This took three months of hiding by day, running by night. She ate what she could find and drank from whatever moving sources of water she could locate. When I remember Bracha's face, with all the lines etched in for the permanent record, I think of the courage and determination her escape and ultimate arrival into Palestine must have taken. Each line, for me, represents another hurdle in her long, arduous and sacrificial struggle to reach the Holy Land.

The long-denied reunion with her husband was a joyous occasion, and they settled in Jerusalem amid the fewer than 100 Bukharan families who had managed to make it there.

Apparently, there were few opportunities for Bukharan musicians or dancers at that time in Palestine. With no other marketable skills to offer, the Eliezerov brothers' act split up. Bracha and her husband had no choice but to work at a variety of low-paying jobs, including entry-level positions in what we today would call the garment industry.

After a year and a half in Jerusalem, they moved to Tel Aviv, where this rapidly developing city offered more work and better pay. Working long hours as a tailor and seamstress, they soon had enough money to open their own clothing factory, where they produced all types of garments, including ornate and elaborately embroidered Bukharan raiment. To augment their income, Bracha's husband worked as a cantor (a religious singer) in a synagogue.

During this happiest and most productive period in their marriage, Bracha bore two sons. Twins were born to her a few years later. Sadly, the male twin died at birth, but the girl survived.

For about fifteen years, while the clothing business flourished and the Eliezerov children were in school, music was the major interest the family shared. Thus, when Bracha's husband passed away and the factory was closed, the children were able to work as part-time musicians, playing a variety of instruments at such functions as weddings and bar mitzvahs (rites of passage when Jewish boys reach the age of thirteen and one week and assume responsibility for their own religious education).

In 1962, the three youngsters formed a musical act and launched a career that has proven to be so successful that they continue to perform together to this day.

Since her children are either touring Europe or busy with their own families, Bracha's life is now largely confined to the microcosm of her Tel Aviv apartment. For the most part, she seems to be sustained by her musical recordings, her television set and the memorabilia that surround her. But, as the five deadbolt locks on her door attest, she still feels a stranger in a strange land.

Bracha remains a Bukharan, perhaps the last of the small community of Bukharans who emigrated to Palestine fifty-seven years ago.

"Badouin"
Israel – 1989
Lynda Hoyle Ellis – ©
F.R.S.A.

16

A DESERT BEDOUIN WOMAN

Our subject, fifteen-year-old Chamda Zanoon El Azazme, is a member of the Azazme tribe, one of three major Bedouin clans who have roamed Middle Eastern deserts for some 2,000 years. While the majority of these clans remain in their land of origin, Saudi Arabia, some 350 Azazmes live in the Negev Desert, south of Beer Sheba, in a desolate area known as Yeroham.

The most primitive of all the cultures we encountered, the desert Bedouin's lifestyle is also the most immediately endangered. Traditionally shepherds and hunters, their economic survival has always depended upon the accessibility of vast areas of grazing land. Before 1948, they enjoyed the freedom to roam the Negev and the Sinai deserts, largely ignored by Israel and Egypt alike. But, after the Camp David Accords of 1978, which ceded the Sinai to Egypt and the Gaza Strip to Israel, an unexpected antagonism has developed between the Israeli government and the Bedouin. Israel realized how many acres of precious grasslands were being destroyed by uncontrolled grazing (one Bedouin family requires at least about 1.9 square miles) and declared much of the Negev a natural preserve. Thus denied adequate grasslands to feed their camels, sheep and goats, most of the Bedouin were forced to abandon their nomadic lifestyle and try to find employment in the cities.

Despite concerted efforts by the well-intentioned absorption centers, the disgruntled, unskilled nomads found the transition to urban life difficult. Moved into government-provided housing settlements, they resisted even the most basic demands of adaptation, grudgingly learning rudimentary Hebrew and half-heartedly learning the simpler trades, such as carpentry, masonry and other manual crafts. Only in recent years have the Bedouin availed themselves of the educational opportunities afforded, at no cost, by Israeli schools and universities. But, as the absorptive process proceeds inexorably and the Bedouin are led out of the desert and into the 20th century, one more tile of Israel's mosaic of cultures crumbles – one more color of the rainbow fades.

At the present time, there are but thirty-five desert Bedouin families doggedly clinging to their traditional lifestyle. Each family has been allowed its own small grazing area south of Beer Sheba. Here a few Azazme families persist in scratching out a bare subsistence, proudly clinging to this tranquil way of life, eschewing the uncertainty of starting over in the frenetic city.

By necessity, these families function as a cooperative, with most of the able-bodied men working five days a week for such government-sponsored projects as construction, road-laying and irrigation.

The government, sympathetic to the plight of its desert people, has subsidized the construction of a pipeline which provides water to much of Yeroham, obviating the need for the Bedouin to roam in search of it. In those few spots not serviced by the pipeline, water is provided by tanker trucks.

For the short term, at least, the Azazmes should be able to preserve a semblance of their former independence. However, the anachronistic protrusion of television antennae from their tent roofs signifies that factors other than government-imposed sanctions are, not so slowly, but surely, eroding the sand walls of isolation the tent dwellers hid behind so assiduously for 2,000 years. These factors are the self-imposed impingements of such Westernizing influences as television, the automobile and convenience shopping in the Beer Sheba marketplace. The once-disdained accumulation of material goods has insinuated its way into their lifestyle. But the acquisition of modern conveniences, of course, demands more money than the occasional sale of a few camels can provide. And, just as every once-self-sufficient culture discovers when its expectations are raised and wants become needs, the men of the Azazme tribe have been compelled to forswear their unspoken vows of pastoral languor and enter the urban job market. Interestingly, quite a few Bedouin have discovered that their knowledge of the uncharted desert is a marketable skill, and they have been hired by the Israeli army as trackers.

In effect, despite the few Azazme families who stubbornly proclaim their orthodoxy, the assimilation of the desert Bedouin is nearly complete. The tent enclaves are now more cosmetic than practical. What little animal herding, crop raising and tribal interaction remains has been assumed by the Azazme women and children. Clearly, an era is ending. At any moment, I realized, the Azazmes could fold their tents and vanish, depriving us of a glimpse of this once-great culture. That's why Lunda and I were so anxious to contact them.

Because the desert Bedouin had always skirted the perimeter of civilization, these clever, capable people had never felt compelled to record their history. Instead, what little we know about this ancient culture is apocryphal, handed down from generation to generation in the form of often bizarre parables, as you will read at the end of this chapter.

Through the good services of Dantchu Arnon, an Israeli photojournalist who accompanied us on much of this venture, we were fortunate enough to meet and hire Sefi Hanegbi, who not only arranged for our visit to the Azazme tent, but served as our guide and translator. Sefi is an enterprising camel trader who organizes camel safaris in Eilat, the southernmost part of Israel. Apparently impressed with the importance of our project, he must have communicated these feelings to the Azazmes with all the fervor of a used-camel salesman. At any rate, after an adventuresome hour-and-a-half trip by car (as described in the "Diary" chapter), we were pleasantly surprised by the warm greeting we received. Later we were to learn that desert tradition assures even an enemy of such hospitality when he visits a Bedouin tent. But, at the time, we felt quite special as they literally rolled out the red carpet and ushered us into the family section of the tent, which, according to Sefi, is seldom open to strange men. The other half of the shelter (the *madafeh*) is reserved for men. This is the only room in which coffee is served, since they regard the bitter coffee bean to be a symbol of the bitterness of life, from which the women are to be shielded. After the ritual of grinding the green coffee beans with a brass mortar and pestle, the grounds are boiled in a small amount of water and served in tiny cups. Perhaps this also explains why the ceremonial sipping of coffee is immediately followed by the serving of sweet tea. The Bedouin, however, regard tea as a symbol of the sweeter aspects of life.

Since we were received by women, we were not served coffee, but rather an aromatic tea. Lunda and I must have registered a quizzical look as Chamda rinsed out the semiopaque glasses with a hint of water. My husband, Elisha, who is not only fluent in Arabic but understands Bedouin customs, drew us aside and whispered an admonition I will never forget. Nodding toward the grime-stained glasses, he insisted, "Even if you die today, you will drink your tea!" Needless to say, we saved face for everyone by heeding his warning, not to mention anything about our lives. Only later did we learn that to refuse a Bedouin's hospitality is taken as an insult. To this day I am thankful for having visited the Azazmes during Ramadan, an Islamic period of fasting. As an anthropologist, I have had the dubious honor of being an honored guest at many communal ceremonies in Africa, the Middle East and other emerging Third World nations. For most of these occasions I became an instant vegetarian. I realize it is not a good quality for an anthropologist, but if that is my only bad quality, then so be it.

But back to more pleasant things, such as Bedouin tea, which, appropriate to this discussion, is thought to cure upset stomachs. We found it to be a tasty and refreshing drink. It tasted much like the herbal tea one can buy in America. Sefi, who is conversant in Pataya, the desert dialect, asked Chamda to reveal the source of the aromatic herbs she had brewed. With a straight face she replied, "Wissotzky", which is the Israeli equivalent of "Lipton's"! The supposed medical elements and the piquant taste were added in the form of leaves from a desert plant called *marve hamisholeshet* and the fragrance from indigenous herbs they call *parosheet* and *kochav rechani*.

As you might imagine, our visit drew more than a few visitors from neighboring tents. Many of the items we brought with us, Polaroid cameras, video cameras, tape recorders and Lunda's paraphernalia, were things they had never seen. Diplomatically but firmly, we had to insist that the equipment was not to be touched by inquisitive (and possibly acquisitive) hands.

As soon as she was certain that the obligatory amenities had been properly observed, Lunda posed her shy, giggling subject in the best lighting available. Her legs straddling a makeshift easel, Lunda organized her canvas, palette and brushes and went to work. She was about to tackle what she now remembers as one of the most fascinating but trying painting sessions she'd ever experienced. Every few minutes, Chamda would jump up to look after a typical two-year-old boy, who was her charge. I found it odd that some other woman would not offer to relieve Chamda of this distracting responsibility while she was being sketched, but no one did. What I did observe was that no one attempted to discipline this whining youngster or try to distract him, as I did with every gimmick I could think of. I wonder now if their behavior would have been different had it been a girl. As if this were not enough annoyance to the usually unflappable Lunda, the self-conscious Chamda insisted on covering her mouth with her hand. When we reasoned correctly that she was embarrassed because she was exposing her normally veiled face in the presence of strange men, Lunda sketched around the hand-covered mouth. This accounts for the portrayal of a veiled Chamda in the finished painting.

While Lunda worked, unflustered as always and perhaps even enjoying her performance before the curious Bedouin who crowded behind her, my videotaping efforts were frustrated, with nothing but a mass of *derrieres* filling my viewfinder. Finally, Elisha came to the rescue. He led a few children outside and began taking Polaroid shots of them. This evoked such squeals of delight that most of Lunda's audience raced out to see Elisha's "magic" act. Now they all wanted their pictures taken. Luckily, we had brought along enough film to satisfy their requests – and allow me to record and videotape the anthropological information I needed.

Here are my observations, based on what I saw and what I learned from interviewing the extremely cooperative elder members of this Azazme family.

The desert wind whistled through the tent, keeping us relatively dry and cool, despite an outside temperature of around 120 degrees. Chickens strutted in and out, pecking at seeds placed in round, battered tin pans for them. Hanging from the roof of the tent were leather (goatskin) sacks of goat milk. In the absence of refrigeration, milk stored in such a manner does not sour, for reasons I leave for biochemists to ponder. The Bedouin summer tents are made from stitched-together burlap sugar sacks. The winter tents, to protect the family and its smaller animals from the extreme cold and strength of desert winds, are constructed from stoutly sewn-together goatskins. Given the scarcity of fuel, let alone heating utilities, the only warmth is provided by extra blankets and whatever heat is generated by the goats and sheep they let into their tents at night.

Traditionally, the basic diet of the Bedouin consists of dairy products made from goats, sheep and camels during the "birthing" season. These foods are called *labna* and *samna*. Out of season, they subsist primarily on a hard cheese (*laban kishk*), which they form into small balls. These are then crushed and mixed with water, either to be eaten directly or flavored with herbs and cooked. Their bread (not unlike pita bread) is made from locally grown wheat. The grain is stone ground, formed into flat ovals and cooked on a large, flat pan atop a crude iron stand, which is fueled by whatever dried sticks or twigs they can find among the sparse desert growth.

Only on a few special occasions do the Bedouin eat meat. However, since their recent discovery of Beer Sheba's modern supermarkets, they augment their diet with rice, sweet peas, frozen chickens, eggs and, as a special treat, chocolate paste. Regrettably, their ingestion of richer foods, especially sugar-laden items, has introduced the hitherto unknown problem of tooth decay. The Azazmes still rely on chewing sticks to clean their teeth and massage their gums. It is hoped they overcome their reticence or aversion to visiting Beer Sheba's free health facilities. If not, they seem destined to suffer the same periodontal problems most Westerners do.

It would not have been considered in good taste to discuss matters of religion, Bedouin mores or especially personal hygiene during our visit, since all my questions and their answers would have had to be translated by a male outsider, Sefi. But later investigation through female interrogators provided most of the following information.

As is true of most Middle Eastern cultures, the desert Bedouin are patriarchal. The elder males of each clan, tribe or family enjoy implicit autocratic powers, although they seldom abuse them. Actually, the men behave responsibly and lovingly toward their women and children, even helping their wives with the more menial domestic chores.

The few Azazme men who choose not to commute to Beer Sheba for work spend their waking hours either herding their camels or socializing with other men in the *madafeh*. And now that Israeli and Jordanian television programs are available to them, it comes as no shock that the Bedouin are as involved in the story of "Dynasty" as any other countryman. The Bedouin traditionally do not believe in doing more work than is necessary, but they do take care of their families and provide them with the necessities.

At night, the entire family sleeps in the family room, on rolled out single mattresses. Apparently, when the husband's libido demands sexual intercourse, he merely crawls in with his wife and makes love with her, undeterred by the presence of the children. To Western mores, this practice may seem to be primitive. In the other sense of the word, it is essential, not only to satisfy connubial needs of the participants, but in some ways to the edification of the onlookers. Also, I would imagine, it precludes the need for those embarrassing birds-and-bees stories that most Western parents feel compelled to tell their children, who patiently wait for their parents to get it off their chests. When our youngest son began taking an interest in females, Elisha had travelled to West Africa and was not due to return for a minimum of three months. I felt it incumbent upon me to take over this "fatherly" duty and explain sexuality to the boy. When I told him that I thought we should have a talk about sex, his reply was, "Sure Mom, what do you want to know?"

Unlike the urbanized Bedouin, who enjoy the luxury of hot and cold running water in their dwellings, the desert Bedouin we visited are "dry campers". With no evidence of indoor plumbing or portable toilets, one can only assume that slit trenches serve as their waste receptacles.

The desert Bedouin, after 2,000 years of living in a condition of perennial drought, have an innate respect for water and a respect for the preservation of the few natural resources still available to them in the desert. Even though it has been made abundantly available to them by pipeline and tanker trucks, they still consider water their most precious resource and continue to collect rainwater. In keeping with this custom of conservation, the use of water for personal hygiene is considered a luxury. However, they wash their hands, feet and faces before prayer, before and after meals and after sexual intercourse. But they recycle their "gray" water by using it to enhance the irrigation of their meager crops.

One of the more positive aspects of the Israeli Absorption Program is the reaching out of socialized medicine to the Bedouin. Desert women, who once bore their children unattended or with the help of a friend (midwives were unavailable except in the larger tribes), are now opting to deliver their children in hospitals. The resultant drop in infant mortality has been dramatic.

One could hardly describe the desert Bedouin as ascetic. But the fact that the Azazme tribe observed Ramadan by fasting (and not by praying, at least in our presence), indicates that they loosely ascribe to the Moslem faith. As is to be expected among tribes with no knowledge of the written language, their religious tenets are only vaguely orthodox and, in the absence of mosques and mullahs, informal in practice. Yet the Bedouin (especially the women) remain as unquestioning of Islam as they are of their many superstitions and, as increasing numbers of young Bedouin attend school and learn to read, they have been introduced to the Koran by Arab teachers. This has promulgated an almost born-again fervor among the newly enlightened students. Unfortunately, if we begin to count and identify which Bedouin are becoming enlightened, we would find them to be the urban Bedouin and not those of the desert.

In prior research I had seen breathtaking examples of ancient Bedouin artisanship. Consequently, I had expected to find examples of traditional weaving, embroidery and jewelry in the Azazme tent. But, save for the magnificently embroidered costume (a priceless heirloom) Chamda wore for the occasion, I found none. It is reasonable to assume that, given the opportunity to purchase reasonably accurate, machine-made facsimiles of the impeccable needlecraft for which Bedouin women were once famous, hand embroidery is a vanishing art, another victim of modernization. Oh, there remain a few embroiderers who will do custom work, I was told, but at a price only the wealthy can afford. I have observed this cross-culturally. Those societies who relied on their handicraft for subsistence, and who still pursue their crafts as their only skill, have been exploited by entrepreneurs, who buy the native work for pennies and sell them for huge profits. I do not mean to demean or blame these people, but I do feel that a more equitable arrangement should be made in the interests of the cultures involved. Even in our country, handwork for the most part has become a thing of the past. One cannot pay for the hours and dedication to the craft that it truly deserves. We have become a nation of obsolescence. It does not pay to repair something as it is cheaper to simply replace the item. So, too, has it become untenable for the Bedouin to continue in their intricate and magnificent embroidery.

The Western clothing adopted by the younger men had been bought in Beer Sheba. But this concession to homogenization is understandable. Just imagine how ludicrously impractical it would be for a high-rise roofer to report for work in a billowing kaftan!

Other than the simple designs painted on their two storage chests, we saw nothing to indicate that the Azazmes produced or collected graphic art. But, come to think of it, how could you hang a painting on a tent wall? Also, when you consider the very nature of nomadic (roaming) life, the concept of settling down in one spot is a contradiction. The impermanence of the Bedouin's home sites would seem to dictate that the accumulation of non-essential goods would be impractical. Of course, with the imposition of land conservancy laws, which restrict their mobility, plus the outreach of civilization to the Negev, the tents of Yeroham may very well be replaced with hard-wall housing developments. I remind the reader of the development of desert areas such as Palm Springs and Las Vegas in the United States. Should this be the case, the desert Bedouin will become "Suburbanite" Bedouin in spite of themselves.

Outside the tent, a young girl of about nine years was trying to play some traditional Bedouin music on a homemade flute. The instrument was nothing more than a fourteen-inch piece of half-inch pipe, with eight holes drilled along its length. She seemed pleased that I would come outside to listen to her earnest efforts, and I was honestly impressed by the whistle-like sounds she coaxed from that scrap of iron plumbing. Without benefit of a mouthpiece, she positioned the tube on her lower lip and blew across the open top, while her nimble fingers flitted over the holes. Not only was the melody discernible, but the harmony was quite pleasing to my ear. I applauded when she finished and gave this sweetheart of a child a hug. Then, as if on some anachronistic cue, I heard the sound of an Israeli rock'n'roll band in the distance. At first I thought someone was playing our car radio. But when a teenage boy appeared around the tent corner, holding a radio-cassette player "boom box" in one hand, while the other held a stick to direct the camels, I could only shake my head and laugh in disbelief. If ever there could be a perfect embodiment of my thesis, this boy was it. From his Nike shoes to his Levi jeans, even to his jazzy tee-shirt and floppy hat, this boy was as "totally rad" as any high-schoolers you might find in an American mall.

In the absence of a written history, the lore of the desert Bedouin exists only in the form of fables, which have been passed on from father to son (and mother to daughter) for 2,000 years. Although they have been embellished in the retelling process, I must believe these parables retain their original *raisons d'etre*: to dramatize basic Bedouin virtues, such as honor, caution (meaning the avoidance of haste) and loyalty. Here are three examples.

A story from Razan min Nishatan, a Bedouin storyteller, explains that doing things in haste comes from the devil. The story is about one man whose fire went out. His wife asked him to go the long distance to the neighboring family to bring an ember to rekindle their fire. He went to the closest neighbor (about 500 yards). While the Bedouin walked slowly across the desert floor at night, a caravan passed, and the man spent a long time exchanging stories with them. The caravan had come from Damascus, Syria, and they were now on their way to Cairo, Egypt. The man became very excited and asked if he could join them. They agreed, and after several weeks they arrived in Cairo. The man then left the caravan to see what Cairo was all about. He spent several months enjoying the sights and just having a good time.

One day, he began to miss his home and his tribe very much. He had the good fortune to meet up with another caravan heading towards Damascus. After a long period of exchanging greetings and niceties, the man asked if he could join their caravan. They agreed and set off the following morning. After three weeks, they finally reached the place of his tribe. Darkness had already settled on the desert. Without the usual and customary flourish of gratuities, the man hastened away. He was so excited about seeing his family again, he ran all the way in the darkness. Just before entering his tent, he remembered the ember his wife had requested and though his excitement was overwhelming, he sped to his neighbor for the ember. He did not even give the most common salutations, just grabbed the ember and ran. On the way back, the man fell into a hole, hurt himself from the fall and burned himself from the ember. The man got up, cleaned himself off, picked up the ember which had almost gone out and remarked that speed is from the devil.

Another traditional story deals with Bedouin honor. The *Tiara* is the name for a gathering for a feast or other special occasion. When the Bedouin gather for the *Tiara*, the men sit together and the most embarrassing thing for anyone to do is to pass gas. This important feast took place and everyone from a large tribe arrived for the Tiara at the gathering place. All the important men from the tribe were sitting together around the fire. During an unusual lull in the conversation, one man passed gas. It was so loud it was even heard by the women. The man turned as red as a tomato. He rose and began to walk. He walked for days, nights and weeks until he was a long distance from his tribe and every one who might have heard. There he found a place and lived alone. His life was quite miserable for the many years he stayed in isolation. After so many miserable years he felt that perhaps his family forgot what he did. He began his trek back home, going very slowly and taking a long time. When he approached the territory of his tribe he hid until he saw a herd of goats with a small boy behind them. He called the boy and asked him from which tribe he came. As it happened, it was the same tribe of the fugitive. He then asked the young boy if he ever heard the name Mohammed Ibn Ibrahim, his own name. The lad replied that he never heard this name before. Mohammed then asked the lad his age. The boy replied that he didn't know exactly, but he was born three years before the big gas explosion.

Sefi told a story about a friend of his whose job it was to research areas in the desert for ancient tombs or relics, before any construction could take place. One day his friend came to him and told him he was going to Wadi Paran because the government wanted to put in water tanks. Sefi volunteered to go with him and, at the Wadi, they met a Bedouin named Salman. They exchanged greetings, drank some coffee and generally asked Salman many questions about the Wadi, and what he knew of the area that might assist them in locating any holy places. Throughout the questioning however, Sefi and his friend felt something was wrong with Salman. When they questioned him he reported that last night he saw Ahbed, known to the Bedouin as a Bedouin black slave. He said that only yesterday Ahbed ran after him when he tried to remove a stone from the cave where he thought Ahbed and his mistress were buried. In the morning, nothing was there, so he was quite concerned. Now to understand this fear, one must first hear the story of Ahbed.

Salman tells the story as he heard it around the time he was in kindergarten. The tale is about Salachadin. During the Moslem period, Salachadin was a great Moslem general who conquered the Middle East from the Crusaders. Salachadin crossed Wadi Paran, saw there was plenty of water and decided to camp there for a couple of days. Young girls walking their herds in the day would come at night to bring the great general warm goat's milk to drink and in the morning a cup of cold goat's milk would be left for him. One morning, someone stole his cup of milk. It was very embarrassing. How could such a great general tell anyone that someone would dare steal his milk? The second morning, the same thing happened and again he couldn't bring himself to tell anyone. He began to get very nervous. When it happened on the third morning, he finally asked one of his officers if he knew who drank his milk. The officer did not know who would do such a thing, but after the fifth occurrence, Salachadin ordered three of his officers to stand watch over his milk through the night. He instructed them to catch the thief of his milk and if they were not successful on the sixth night they would all have to die. Salachadin went to sleep while his officers sat around the milk waiting. With the first light of the morning, they saw a very large black man, whose size belies any description. He walked directly to the cup of milk and, in one gulp, finished its contents. All the officers jumped to grab him. It was Ahbed, a very rich Bedouin but lowly officer in Salachadin's army. When Salachadin questioned Ahbed about the milk, Ahbed replied that he had an agreement with Salachadin's wife. The agreement was that if Ahbed could steal Salachadin's milk for seven days, then she would leave him and go to Ahbed. Needless to say, Salachadin was astonished. His wife had so much money and worldly goods, how could she think of leaving him for Ahbed. Salachadin then went to confront his wife? She admitted to the plan she had with Ahbed, and Salachadin went back to Ahbed. He told him that he could take his wife since only one day separated them, but both of them would go without heads. The two were decapitated and put into a grave in Wadi Paran. Salman tried to find the grave.

The Azazme tribe, the one we visited, are very bitter. They say there is a lot of jewelry and a very big fort in this area. They cautioned Salman not to go to that place because Ahbed is still very angry that Salachadin killed him. But Salman said he didn't believe that and was sure he could find the riches and jewelry supposedly buried there. But, you see, even after an attempt, he couldn't bring himself to do it, and no water tanks were put in that area.

That Salman, a university student, is unable to distinguish fact from fantasy attests to Bedouin belief in some measure of truth in every parable that no Bedouin is willing to test.

A DRUZE SHEIK

Sheik Adel Mefleh Halaby is one of the most respected Druze in the village of Daliat el-Carmel. Not only is he a revered religious leader, but he is an eminently successful businessman. He owns and operates a popular restaurant and a gift shop which features Druze handicrafts.

We were privileged to be invited into Mr Halaby's elegant home for the sitting, and although I felt constrained from interviewing the sheik about the Druze religion, I found him to be a most gracious host. In deference to Lunda, who, I could see, was finding it difficult to get the voluble patriarch to hold still for more than a few seconds, I moved to the living room, where I interviewed one of Mr Halaby's nephews, a teacher in a neighboring Druze village, Usafia, who was asked to come specifically to answer my questions. I had seen rooms like this in Africa, I realized. Along all four walls were sofas and chairs of various types, suggesting that the room was used for the reception and entertainment of many guests. The only adornments on the walls were photographs of the sheik meeting with dignitaries from many different countries. His most prized possession sat in the middle of the room. It was a large and ornate replication of a tree with mother-of-pearl leaves, imported from the Philippines.

When Lunda had finished her sketching and I had finished my interview and videotaping, the women in our group were invited into a special room which I dubbed "The Ladies Room". Lunda and I, Ruth Dayan, Nomi Arnon and her daughter were joined by the sheik's wife and several of his daughters and daughters-in-law. We sat on cushions placed on the floor along three walls of the room. Although I enjoyed the refreshments we were served and the chitchat with the Druze ladies, I could not help wishing I were in the living room, where Elisha and the Halaby men were having a gay old time, judging from the laughter I could hear. But, as is true in almost all Moslem families, the Druze social order places women in a position of subservience to men, and the Western concept of equality for women is totally foreign to them. The implicit dominance of the male was made undeniably explicit when some of the younger boys showed me the framed family tree hung on one wall. As they proudly pointed to their names on the chart, I was somewhat taken aback to notice that only the names of the male Halabys appeared on the tree!

The role of a Druze woman is rigidly prescribed by tradition. She is expected never to work outside the home, which is considered her primary area of responsibility. She is responsible for raising the children, preparing meals and keeping the home clean and in order. Although she is expected to marry at an early age, anywhere between seventeen and twenty, she has few opportunities to meet young men. That is because of the strict social restrictions imposed upon her. She is not allowed to attend social events, such as school dances, and her only chance to meet anyone outside of her immediate family is at family weddings. Consequently, her mate is most often selected for her. Usually he will be a young Druze man from the same village, sometimes even from within the family. Interfaith marriage is forbidden, and a dowry is required. This is usually in the form of clothing, bed linen and jewelry. The groom is obliged to make a financial agreement with the bride's family.

Until recently, the typical Druze couple would produce six children. But now that number has decreased somewhat, probably because Western ideas concerning family planning have been disseminated throughout Israel.

Divorce among the Druze is unusual, but the most cited grounds are female infertility and the inability of the woman to bear male offspring. Druze marriages are monogamous, and the bearing of sons is so important that, even if the wife has given birth to several daughters, divorce is deemed mandatory because she has failed to produce a son. Civil law regarding marriages, divorce and inheritance is administered by Druze lawyers and religious leaders, who are held in high esteem by the community.

Along with the great respect the religious leaders are accorded comes a separate, more stringent code of behavior, dress and mores than what is expected of the Druze laity. Because positions of religious leadership are so highly respected, the requirements for obtaining this ranking are quite rigid. A candidate for this high office must study for years, pass many tests of secrecy and loyalty and ascribe to a dress code that demands they wear specific clothing that will not draw attention to them. More specifically, he must never wear bright colors, his head must be covered with a white cloth (or turban) and his tunic must be an unadorned black dress. He may not smoke, drink alcoholic beverages or use offensive language. In other words, he must be the perfect role model for his constituency. I was told that every boy, until the age of sixteen, can look through the religious books at will and visit the holy places. After age sixteen, he needs permission from religious leaders. He is also then responsible for himself and expected to behave as any other religious man, which means to wear the traditional Druze costume, grow a mustache, shave his head entirely, and visit the praying house on a regular basis. To become a part of the inner circle, an individual must not have broken any of the Ten Commandments, which are sacrosanct to them. If even one of the commandments was broken, the person could only be accepted as high as the second religious position. The first position entitles the religious person to read from the Da'Wa, literally "the Divine Word", which is one of the holiest books for the Druze. The second position allows the individual to read only explanations or interpretations of this book. This rule applies to the lifetime of the person. Unlike the Jews and Christians, the Druze cannot atone for their sins and be forgiven. On Judgment Day, God will decide whether the individual can go to Heaven or Hell. If a religious person commits a crime or breaks any commandment, he immediately becomes a non-religious person and cannot come to religious houses again for prayer.

I was told that, on rare occasions, women have been chosen to be religious leaders, which struck me as an odd exception to traditional Druze attitudes toward females. Not every Druze can become a religious leader or even what they consider an educated or initiated person. A candidate, male or female, must have exhibited some signs to the community that he or she is intelligent and capable of secrecy and loyalty.

Druze religious services are conducted on Thursday evenings in inconspicuous halls, devoid of decoration, although I assume they employ some form of lectern to hold their holy books. A service is composed of two parts. The first part, which is open to all comers, is devoted to discussions of community affairs and other secular matters. Afterwards, the uninitiated and/or unenlightened people must leave before the praying, studying and meditation begin.

Each Druze community has its own designated religious leader. For generations, the spiritual leader of all the Druze in Israel has been a member of the Tarif family, headquartered in the western part of the Galil. The leadership is a hereditary position, rather than an elected one.

To try to understand the Druze religious beliefs and why they are so secretive about them, it is necessary to go back in history to the latter part of the 10th century. According to my sources, that is when the religion was founded in Cairo, Egypt, by an Islamic dissident, Fatimid Imam-Khalif Al-Hakim bi' Amrillah. You will understand if I refer to him simply as Al-Hakim or the Khalif from here on. The Khalif and his followers were members of the Shia' sect of Islam, more specifically, the Isma'ili Shia's of Egypt. In the 10th century, power struggles and quests for Messianic rule were raging throughout Islam.

The Druze believed that Al-Hakim was the true Messiah. Consequently, when disagreements arose between them and the Sunni branch of Islam over who should assume the successive powers of the Prophet Mohammed, Al-Hakim and his constituents built their own mosque in Cairo. It was completed around 1013 CE. The Shia's insisted that the succession should be patrilineally inherited through the Prophet's sons. The Sunnis disagreed vehemently, and since they were in the majority, persecuted all the followers of Shia'ism until the last khalif, Al-Muntazar, was either killed or disappeared. The decimated Shia's, fearing eventual extermination, went underground and have remained secretive and isolated from the traditional tenets of Islam ever since.

After Al Muntazar's disappearance (or death), the remaining Shia's placed all matters of faith and morals in the hands of theologians (imams), whom they designated as their intermediaries with God. Such was their faith in the imams that the Shia's believed they could perform miracles. Christian mysticism impacted on their theology to the extent that they believed their religious leaders should be martyred. As opposed to the Shia's, the conservative Sunnis followed the leadership of khalifs, whom they did not imbue with the power to communicate with the deity.

At the height of Al-Hakim's reign, he appointed Hamza Al-Zuzani and Muhammad Al-Darazi, two devoted disciples, to positions of great trust. It was Hamza's mission to spread the divine word (Da'Wa) throughout Al-Hakim's empire (called the Fatamid empire). Darazi's responsibility was to spread the religion beyond the empire, and he has been credited with having spread Druzism to southern Lebanon. It has been speculated that the word Druze is a derivation of Darazi's name.

After a year, Hamza and Darazi fell out. Apparently, Hamza wanted Al-Hakim declared the Messiah, with himself elevated to imam. Darazi refused to agree to this. Then they argued about the proper method to solicit for converts to their depleted ranks. According to my sources, Hamza contended that conversions should be voluntary and based on sound reasoning, whereas Darazi proposed the use of force. The overzealous Darazi is said to have been assassinated in 1019 CE, and later was regarded an heretic by the Druze.

Two years later, Al-Hakim disappeared. Again, it is unclear as to whether he was murdered or went into hiding. Some Druze believe he went to China. Whatever the reason for his disappearance, it motivated Hamza to go into hiding for six years.

The new khalif, Al-Zahir, apparently reverting to the conservative beliefs of the pre-Hakim Shia's, denounced the Druze contention that their imams had a direct connection with the Deity. He threatened anyone who dared continue to so believe. He was ruthless in his pursuit of the defiant Druze and nearly eradicated them. Upon hearing of this, Hamza sent a message to one of his disciples, Baha' Al-Din, urging him to continue teaching from the Da'wa and to spread the endangered faith in Hamza's absence. Al-Din began proselytizing, sending out missionaries and carrying out the dictates of the Da'wa. For approximately sixteen years, along with the few theologians who had survived Al-Zahir's persecutions, he worked on coding the arcane religious tenets of Druzism. The 111 Epistles, composed by Al-Hakim, Hamza and Baha' Al-Din (the last of which Al-Din wrote in 1043 CE) were collected and arranged to comprise the official Canon of the Druze. The Canon consists of six books, all of them so mysteriously encoded that only a select few Druze intellectuals are able to understand their contents. The coding was done intentionally so that, in the event the books fell into the hands of adversaries or strangers, they would be indecipherable.

From the time the last Epistle was written, signalling the closing of the Da'Wa, the principles of the faith (called *Tawid,* meaning oneness of God) have been kept secret and sacrosanct. As mentioned earlier, only a select few members are educated in the Da'wa, and it is through their loyalty to one another that the secrets of the faith are preserved and passed on. The unenlightened Druze are taught a moral and ethical code of behavior. This is the limit of their catechizing, and the faithful never seem to question the fact that they are denied access to the six holy books.

With the closing of the Da'Wa, it was decreed that, henceforth, no one could convert to Druzism. This was based on the conviction that the number of members was fixed at the time of the closing. Their numbers are said to remain constant because the Druze believe in metempsychosis, which holds that when one member dies, another is born to take his place and the dead soul enters the body of the newborn.

The tracing of the Druze racial background is as complicated and mystery-shrouded as their religion. Their physical appearance is unlike the typical (if there is such a thing) Middle Easterner. I am reminded of the looks of the Circassians, with a lighter complexion and varying facial characteristics. One encyclopedia described their religion as a cross between Christianity and Islam.

Not feeling qualified to evaluate that assertion, I can only present those facts made available to me, leaving the reader to categorize the Druze *vis-a-vis* the traditional Moslems. Although they share a common language, Arabic, their codes of law are completely different. The Moslems follow the Five Pillars of Islam which dictate such practices as: compulsory prayer five times a day facing Mecca, the center of their universe; acknowledging no god but Allah and the prophet Mohammed; charity; fasting all day during the month of Ramadan; and, if possible, a pilgrimage to Mecca. The Druze code of law consists of seven duties: a belief in monotheism and the recognition of Al-Hakim as the center of their worship; the rejection of any teachings but Druze; the rejection of Satan and non-believers; the unquestioning acceptance of God's acts; total submission to Him no matter what; and honesty, mutual cooperation and solidarity between fellow Druze.

Resorting to the anthropological method of comparing and contrasting, the following lists will illustrate some other differences between Druzism and Islam:

Druzism	Islam
Promises a beatific vision of the Holy One as the reward for goodness; Hell is the punishment for failing to achieve the status of a just man.	Promises Paradise of earthly delights.
Predestination, according to His cosmic plan.	Predestination is a cardinal Islamic concept. According to the Koran, if you die for your country, you are a martyr.
There is no rite of passage regarding circumcision. It is practiced for hygienic purposes but without any ceremony.	Moslems believe in circumcision.
Polygamy is forbidden.	Polygamy is permitted.

Divorce is a complex matter, difficult to obtain. It can be initiated by male or female.	Divorce is very easy and usually only initiated by males.
Druze women have always had the right to own property and to dispose of it at will.	Moslem women have no such rights.

A student of comparative religions can see that there are enough common threads between the Druze, Islam and Christianity to support the theory that, despite their sharp differences with the other two faiths, the Druze fall somewhere in between these other religions.

The Druze have their own flag of five colors – green, red, yellow, blue and white. Each color symbolizes one of their major prophets. The most renowned Druze prophet, Itro, was buried near Tiberias, Israel. Every April 25, the Druze make a pilgrimage to this holy place. Itro (or Jethro) is mentioned in the Bible (Exodus 18:17-22). He was Moses' father-in-law, and one source said he gave Moses the magic walking stick which was later used to part the Red Sea, but I cannot corroborate that information. It is documented that Moses was physically and emotionally drained from acting as the sole administrator of all his people. He was counselled by the sagacious prophet Itro to delegate some of his responsibilities to others. Moses took Itro's advice, thus lessening his workload and allowing himself to concentrate on his role as chief justice. This incident is cited as being the basis for the tables of organization of all hierarchical groups as we know them today.

Because the Druze value secrecy and inconspicuousness so highly, as mentioned earlier, they choose not to erect temples, cathedrals or churches. Nor do they openly congregate very often. Other than their Thursday meetings, religious duties are left to each enclave's religious leader. (You may have noticed that these leaders avoid the appellation priest, rabbi or minister. This, along with their insistence upon inconspicuous attire, is consistent with their penchant for secrecy.) The Holy Place in Daliat el Carmel is called Abu Ibrahim, after the prophet, and has existed for many hundreds of years. In the neighboring village of Usafia, the Holy Place is called Abu Abdullah. From what I could gather, Daliat's religious leader makes several visits every week to both Holy Places. Possibly to maintain a low profile, he shuns traveling by conveyance and walks to these locations. His path to Usafia is always through the fields, never along the main thoroughfare, which is probably the shorter route.

Although present-day Daliat's population of 12,000 is 95 percent Druze and 5 percent Moslem, the Druze continue to maintain the strictest secrecy in all matters pertaining to their arcane religion. One need not look back very far in history to discover the reason for this. Before 1948, Daliat was a small village of 600 Druze. It was surrounded by many Moslem villages. Because of the intense rivalry between the two Islamic sects, the Sunnis and Shiites, the Moslems blamed the Druze "infidels" for any problems that arose. But on the several occasions when they launched raids on the vastly outnumbered Druze, the latter defended themselves with a ferocity that demoralized their attackers and drove them off. Incredibly, the Druze army consisted of a mere handful of horsemen armed with swords and knives.

What makes the Druze warrior such a fearless combatant is his belief that, at the moment of his birth, the prescribed date, time and method of his death is determined. As Israeli and Lebanese military leaders were surprised to learn, this belief in predestination is so ingrained in the Druze that they fight with matchless courage, never concerned with the possibility of an untimely death.

Druze legend has it that there have been instances of divine intervention on their behalf. An apocryphal tale relates that on one fateful day the Moslems attacked a small Druze village. Their intent was to slay all the Druze men and capture the women. In the face of certain defeat by the Moslem horde, the Prophet Ibrahim appeared to the Druze and led them to a resounding victory. As I noted in the "Desert Bedouin" chapter, in the unwritten history of a culture it is difficult to separate fact from fable. Yet most of these tales often contain more than a grain of truth.

Another Druze legend may help explain why orthodox Druze go to doctors only on those occasions when they need pain-killing medication. The story tells of a sheik who lived alone and unmarried. Around his house were many grapevines and fruit-bearing trees. He worked the soil with his hands and made it into the nicest area in the land. He also had many sheep, goats and chickens and believed that people were meant to live this way, praying to a higher being and finding themselves through religion. One day he fell ill, but did not want to see a doctor. The villagers forced him to, however, and the doctor performed an operation upon the unwilling patient. When the sheik returned to his home, he died.

Prior to 1948, illiteracy was endemic among the Druze, as it was among the Bedouin and many other cultures comprising the mosaic sects in the land of Israel. In those days, one man from among the few literate Druze was chosen to be the *muchtar* (leader). Only this one person was able to read letters sent to his village. Because of this, the *muchtar* was the most powerful and respected man in his community. After 1948, when Israel opened elementary schools in all the villages, the Druze children gradually learned to read and write. As they mastered these skills, the community came to rely less on the *muchtar* and more on the newly-literate children to do their reading.

Until 1960-61, only a few Druze children finished high school. But from 1963, when a group of Druze children began being bussed to high school in Haifa (the closest high school to them), until the present, they have all availed themselves of government-provided secondary schools and universities.

Perhaps because of their biblical link to the Jews, their industriousness and their strong religious convictions, the Druze are faced with few of the problems that many of the immigrating cultures are experiencing. Granted the right to conduct their own judicial system (in all but criminal matters), the orthodox Druze have not had to undergo the often painful process of absorption into the social pattern.

However, the exposure of the younger generation to other cultures has resulted in some instances of interfaith marriages. A tale was related to me on this subject as well, to emphasize the Druze' attitude towards intermarriages. I was told that a friend of my interviewee from high school wanted to study medicine in a university in Jerusalem. His father was very excited as he antici-pated the respect he would receive in the village when his son returned. The father worked very hard, selling furniture, often working until midnight to earn the money required to pay for medical school. After two years of studying, the son fell in love with a Christian girl. He knew his parents would never accept her, so secretly married her and built a house. She bore two daughters without his family even knowing he was married. By chance, the parents heard about it and, of course, raised strong objections, begging their son to divorce her and return to the village to take a Druze bride who would give him sons. The son did not agree, finished medical school and moved to the Beer Sheba area to practice. The villagers were beside themselves because this boy had also been a religious, traditional boy, who could no longer return to a Druze village. The father was so distraught he considered going to Beer

Sheba and killing his son. He did not, but prior to the marriage of his second son, he travelled to Tiberias to pray to Itro and ruminate over what he had done wrong to have caused such a disaster in his family. The father died in Tiberias, and the community feels that he died of a broken heart because of the marriage of his first son.

Intermarriage means excommunication from Druzism, and has caused a great deal of sorrow among the families of the apostates. It is estimated that there are currently about 400 Druze who have intermarried, and it is a fear among Druze that there will be apostasies in ever-increasing numbers as Israel becomes more homogenized.

To that extent, the Druze must be considered an endangered culture.

AN ETHIOPIAN JEWESS

An excess of theories exist regarding the origins of the Ethiopian Jews (Beta Israel, also known as Falashas), as well as when they actually arrived in Ethiopia. What probably adds to this confusion is the fact that the Hebrew bible was and is as important to the Ethiopian Christian as to the Jew. Both Sabbaths are observed, and many Hebraic customs such as purification rites of animals (dietary laws), circumcision of male children on the eighth day after birth, are shared with the entire Ethiopian culture.

Although the religious survival of the Jews depended on many adaptations to Christian Ethiopian culture over the centuries, their economic survival depended on craft specialization, such as pottery, metallurgy, weaving and masonry. A good proportion of Beta Israel were also involved in subsistence farming for absentee landlords. For many years the Falashas had been moving across borders into Kenya and Sudan looking for "greener pastures", work or better living conditions. In Ethiopia, they were not permitted to own land or to use the same water as the Christians, and were subject to higher land taxes and rents than any other ethnic minority group. Because of the prevailing situation of ostracism and persecution, and because it is written in the Torah, the Beta Israel were desperate to get to Jerusalem, especially after 1948.

What is known of the history of the Beta Israel is reflective of most Jews in the Diaspora. There were good times and bad times, periods of plenty and periods of strife. They sequestered themselves in villages in the region of the Semien Mountains. They did this for a couple of reasons: to isolate themselves and thus make themselves less identifiable as Jews, and to make reaching them as difficult as possible. It is said of the Beta Israel that they were fierce warriors in protecting their persons and religion. Attention was first drawn to Beta Israel in the latter part of the 19th century. Joseph Halevy, who was a Jewish orientalist, travelled to Ethiopia in 1867 under the auspices of the Alliance Israelite Universelle. His purpose in going was to determine if, indeed, these people were Jews and to obtain information about them. Halevy wanted to establish Jewish schools in Ethiopia, but the Alliance Israelite Universelle did not agree. It was not until the beginning of the 20th century that Jacques Faitlovich, a student of Halevy, again visited the Beta Israel under a grant from Baron Edmond de Rothschild. He was instrumental in getting some of the youngsters to study Judaism abroad, but few of them ever returned to their villages to teach. Faitlovich made ardent attempts to draw the attention of world Jewry to the Beta Israel group.

Mussolini's troops put an end to Faitlovich's efforts with the Italian invasion of Ethiopia in 1935-36. In fact, the Italians expelled him and Faitlovich found his way to Palestine. In the beginning of the occupation the Italian attitude was favorable towards the Jews. However, by 1938, Fascist, racist and anti-Semitic laws were passed to inhibit their movement and economic survival of these people. About the same time Ethiopia was liberated from the Italians, Faitlovich returned to continue his work. He is still considered the Father of the Falashas.

Haile Selassie did little for the Falashas, and after he was deposed in 1974 by a revolution, matters did not improve for this group. A Marxist regime emerged and attempts at land reform were made. The idea was to redistribute lands owned by the wealthy and give them to the poor among them the Falashas. This did not work, as it was strongly opposed in the north and the landowners there felt that the only way to keep their property would be to rid themselves of the peasants who needed the land. There are no known figures, but it is believed that during this period called "white terror", hundreds of Jews were killed. The government also wanted to eliminate religion from Ethiopian culture. When they saw the opposition to this proposal, they declared Islam and Coptic Christianity the official religions of Ethiopia. All that accomplished was to subject the Catholics, Protestants, Jews and other ethnic minority religions to further persecution. They were not permitted to practice their religions openly, and often their houses of worship were either destroyed or used for other purposes.

By 1975, Israel ruled that any Falasha who wanted to come to Israel was welcome. But here is the paradox. Since the Jews were so hated, more than any other minority ethnic group, would it not seem reasonable that the Ethiopians would be happy to rid themselves of this group? Major Melaku, the Mayor of the Gondar province, the area with the largest Jewish population, would not allow any of his "subjects" to leave. Led by Major Melaku, excessive persecution was carried out on the Jews. Melaku went as far as to blame them for the 1980 crop failure and the famine that followed.

For the past two decades, the plight of the Ethiopian Jew can only be understood against the unstable political and economic situation prevailing at any given time. It would also be a gross omission to neglect to mention the disastrous drought and famine of 1983 that left about 200,000 Ethiopians dead in its devastating trail.

Emigration to Israel of any considerable number of people began only at the beginning of the 20th century. Approximately 1,400 Ethiopian Jews had reached the shores of the Mediterranean. Two years later, the figure had doubled. As an aftermath of the Yom Kippur war of 1973, Ethiopia broke relations with Israel and forbade emigration. Once the Israeli government realized that the only hope for the Beta Israel's salvation had to come from them, they began to take action. They did not want to harm their already fragile relations with Africa. Since the Camp David Accords in 1978, Israel's relations with Egypt had greatly improved. They approached the late President Anwar Sadat to ask him to speak to President Numeiri of Sudan for permission to evacuate the Beta Israel. Permission was granted on the basis of secrecy. The same applied to the refugees in Kenya, although Israel's relations were fairly good with them. Then, again, it was to be a secret mission. Each country had its own reason for the secrecy. From then on, the Mossad, Israel's intelligence agency, went into action.

Secrecy was also of utmost importance for the Mossad, as it could have meant the loss of their own lives and of those they were attempting to save. There were also several Western Jewish activist groups trying to help, and the Mossad feared interference from them. There had been enough attempts by these activists – some successful, some not – in the past, and it was considered a risk to the Mossad agents and their planned routes. As a result of this interference, the Kenya route was soon closed to the Mossad and the only alternative left them was through Sudan. Over the years, the Mossad operated secretly and successfully. Twice, once in July, 1983, two Hercules transport planes landed near the refugee camps and 400 individuals were airlifted out. The second such airlift took place between six to eight months later. By mid-1984, there were a total of about 6,000 Ethiopian Jews in Israel – but this was not enough. It was also becoming obvious that this project of the Mossad was becoming endangered. Something had to be done and done fast. The Beta Israel soon got the message from what I call the "bush telephone". They began holding lengthy plenary sessions and hoarding foods for the long and arduous trek from the Gondar region in Ethiopia to Sudan, their only chance left. They were undernourished, starving and sick, yet they were determined to get to Jerusalem any way they could. To get to Sudan, they had to leave their own mountain regions, cross the desert with their worldly possessions, hoarded provisions and water on their backs, and cross another mountain range before reaching the Sudanese border. Many died on the way; many became ill with malaria; they were victims of attacks by groups of *shiftas*, who not only took their measly provisions, but their shoes and any other valuables they may have had on them. They also raped many women and girls. The only provision left to these desolate people was their water. This trek took upwards of three weeks. Many of the Beta Israel who had crossed the Sudanese borders successfully were remanded to refugee camps, one in Tewawa and another in Um Raquba (the latter having the largest number of Jews), only to be further persecuted and tortured by other non-Jewish refugee groups. By November, 1984, Falashas from many villages had reached Sudanese refugee camps. Conditions in the camps had become even more intolerable. Their very number frightened Sudanese authorities, as there was a limit to how secretive one could be when one speaks about a large enough group of people. Also, by this time there was a lot of outside pressure from activists and foreign governments (by foreign I mean foreign to Sudan and Ethiopia) because of the drought and famine.

Operation Moses was launched. Bus loads of refugees, the least able to survive the existing conditions in the camps, were taken to Tewawa to board planes waiting at the end of the runway at the airport in Khartoum, bound for Israel. From the end of November, 1984, until the first week of January, 1985, thirty-five such flights were made between Khartoum and Israel. Unfortunately, because of a leak to the newspapers in Israel, Operation Moses came to an abrupt halt. Fortunately, most of the Beta Israel were already in Israel when Prime Minister Peres confirmed the reports and made Operation Moses a *fait accompli.* Many people felt that Peres' confirmation was responsible for Sudan putting an end to the rescue mission.

In fact, this operation brought the number of Ethiopians to Israel around 16,000 individuals. These daring and heroic missions were ceased when the Sudanese government was accused by the Arab League of collaborating with Israel. It would be difficult to guesstimate how many Ethiopian Jews remain in Ethiopia today, but their dream of redemption and reunion with their own people is still alive.

Although I was not privy to Operation Moses or to the extent this activity would lead, I vividly remember my own personal excitement. At the same time, I recall Israel coming under attack by organizations in the us and Canada for not only not doing enough for the Falashas, or quickly enough. In Israel's defense, how could she have responded to these accusations when the whole operation and its ultimate success, depended on it being cloaked in secrecy?

The young lady portrayed here was originally from Gondar province in Ethiopia. Shira Yaasu today is twenty-three years of age, is married and has a beautiful four-year-old daughter, Orit. In 1983, in Ethiopia, she married her husband who, in her words, "worked the land". Her father was a rabbi. Ten years ago (1984) she came to Israel, followed by her husband a few months later. She says she came to Israel because it is written in the Torah. She lives in an absorption center in Safed. During the day she works as a caretaker for older people and her husband works in a furniture factory.

When our subject, Shira, arrived for the sitting she came with a very Western coiffured hairdo. She was "prepared" for the work ahead. Shira was a very difficult subject for Lunda to paint. She seemed impatient, fidgety and obviously not where she wanted to be at that moment. I asked her why she was behaving as though she would run out the door given the first opportunity? She claimed that she is very shy. It was my impression that she had somehow been coerced into sitting for us. As a follow-up on this impression, I asked Shira if I could meet her little daughter when Lunda had finished her sketch. She became visibly very excited and immediately agreed. We drove back with her to the absorption center and she was delighted to present her little girl to us. There was such a metamorphic change in her attitude and behavior it was obvious that the portrait sitting was not her idea and did not meet with her approval. Later on, Lunda and I discussed what we should do about the hairdo. Accuracy for me was of the utmost importance. Upon arrival back in Tel Aviv several days later, we buried ourselves in the archives of the Museum of the Diaspora looking for original hairdos from the Ethiopians upon the Falashas' arrival in Israel, thus the hairdo in the portrait. But, jumping back to Safed, I will have deprived you, the reader, by not telling you something about this holy city.

First of all I think it is imperative to explain that there are many different spellings of the name of the city. As some examples, it can be found written Sfat, Safed, Sefat, Tsfat, and so on. These are various Anglicized translations of the name from Hebrew and Arabic. No one is correct or incorrect; it is a matter of choice. Safed is primarily known as the center for Kabbalism (Jewish mysticism). The study of Kabbalah first began in Safed in Galilee (the northern part of Israel) during the 16th century. There were several scholars who began schools for the study of Kabbalism, but the scholar most known and remembered on this subject was Isaac Luria. He had a profound effect on his students and it was they, not Luria, who recorded his theories and intellectual exponents after his death. This is not to imply that he did nothing, but rather to state that it was his students who recorded the bulk of his revelations. The town is situated in the northern part of Galilee. It is not only a center for the study of Kabbalism, but an artist's colony as well. Orthodox Jews live among non-orthodox Jews and there doesn't appear to be any friction between them. Safed had also been approved by the Ministry of Absorption and the Jewish Agency as an appropriate location for Ethiopian Jewry to settle probably because of its high elevation (similar to the mountains of Ethiopia). There are other enclaves of Ethiopians around the country, including their beloved Jerusalem.

Upon their arrival, the Ethiopians were taught the Hebrew language, and skills to work in the various factories of Safed, and although they were encouraged to adapt to life in Israel, they were also encouraged through a cultural craft center overseen by Miriam Perel, the mother of the mayor, to maintain their own cultural identity through ethnic handicrafts such as weaving and ceramics. Many of the Ethiopians today can be found working in one of Safed's several factories, in addition to three diamond-polishing plants. Much of the credit for the advancement of the city of Safed, its industrialization as well as its charming preservation, goes to Zeev Perel, the youngest elected mayor in Israel.

Some Jewish organizations have joined in the Ethiopian absorption process. As recently as May, 1989, the Organization for Rehabilitation Through Training (ORT), as reported in the May 25 issue of *The Jewish World*, announced its first Ethiopian graduates as industrial technicians after successfully completing courses at the ORT Junior College in Israel. It is not the only time this group helped the Ethiopian Jews. Back in 1980, ORT was allowed to operate in Ethiopia. At first they were very welcome, as they helped not only the Beta Israel, but the entire community by building schools, roads and infrastructures such as water wells. Later the Ethiopians accused ORT of conspiring to smuggle the Jews out of the country and they were asked to leave.

I would like to describe some of our experiences in Safed. We were a convoy of about six people travelling in two cars. We had just left the Samaritans, whose paschal lamb sacrifice was held thirty days after the Jewish Passover celebration because of a leap year in their calendar. We made our way down Mount Gerizim before the Sabbath and after several side trips on the way drove into Safed on May 4, 1988. Preparations were underway for the celebration of Lag B'Omer (the thirty-third day out of forty-nine between the second day of Passover and Shavuot), the only day on which a marriage, haircutting and any merrymaking can be performed. The atmosphere is similar to that of Mardi Gras, and Jews parade through the streets, Torahs raised above their heads, singing and dancing all the way. Groups of schoolchildren, officially off school on this day, were brought to Safed to join in the merrymaking and sang (chorus fashion) songs appropriate to this special day.

The beauty of Safed compels me to describe what it felt like just walking over the veins of ancient cobbled streets. When this town was built, the streets were designed for camels, donkeys, horses and people. No car could make its way through the winding and narrow streets. A motorcycle could, but then that is also about the width of a donkey! As I walked, my feet hugged the stones. The town silently begged me to peer into doors left ajar, into arched alleyways and up at the windows of the homes untouched since antiquity. A small, hand-painted sign with an arrow pointed the way to the Yosef Karo synagogue. I wondered why such a small, insignificant sign pointed to such an important shrine in Jewish history. Yosef Karo is credited for writing the Shulchan Aruch. In the most simple definition, the Shulchan Aruch is a compilation of an ethical code of behavior for Jews. Very orthodox Jews and the Hassidic Jews (ultra-orthodox) abide by these codes.

To say that I was transported back in time would be an understatement. While on my sole journey through Safed, I was reliving biblical times. What made it even more dramatic were all the Hassidic Jews rushing passed me. It was as though I was one of Isaac Luria's students, but I was the only one walking to the lesson. That Safed has been kept traditionally is a tribute to the people who reside there and if anyone travels to Israel, this town should be close to the top of the list of priorities. It is mentioned not only in the Old Testament, but in the New Testament as well.

A HASSIDIC RABBI

Abraham is a clerical member of perhaps the most controversial movement in Judaism – Hassidism. He was extremely timorous about sitting for Lunda and refused to be videotaped, citing a Biblical remonstration which warns that man was created in God's image and that image must not be duplicated. Fortunately for us, he convinced himself that an oil portrait was not a duplication. He came from his home in Jerusalem to Dantchu's studio in Tel Aviv to pose and be interviewed. When Abraham would not reveal his surname, I gathered that he risked censure from his superiors and constituents if it ever became known that he had allowed his likeness to be painted.

To understand the history of Hassidism, one must know something about the history of Poland, where the movement originated. Other sects under the umbrella of Hassidism arose in other countries, but we will concentrate on the Polish Hassidim. We will return to Abraham and his family in a later discussion.

With the exception of the former Soviet Union, Poland was the largest and most populous country in Europe. It fits neatly between Lithuania, Byelarus and Ukraine on its eastern border, the Czech and Slovak republics to the south, and Germany to the west. Its strategically important north coast is on the beautiful Baltic Sea. It is her geographic position that has made Poland so extremely vulnerable throughout its long and often sordid history.

The country's name is a derivative of a Slavic tribe who called themselves Polanes, meaning plain or field. The Polanes inhabited the land in around 2000 BCE. The name may have been adopted because it also describes the general topography.

There was no documented history of Poland before 900 CE, but it is generally believed that several Slavic tribes united under the dominant Polanes around 800 CE, and became the forefathers of the modern Poles.

The first rulers of Poland were the Piast family. This dynasty reigned and flourished until the last of the Piast monarchs died in 1370. Beginning this era under the leadership of Mieszko I, the Polish domain was composed of two areas. The first section consisted of the strip which borders on the Vistula River and describes an S-shaped course beginning at the Gulf of Danzig (leading into the Baltic Sea) in the north and snakes its way southward along the Western Carpathian Mountains into Czechoslovakia. The second section paralleled the Oder River, which began in the north coastal lowlands of the Baltic Sea and extended southward around the Sudetes Mountains, again into Czechoslovakia.

Mieszko's son, Boleslaw I, conquered parts of Czechoslovakia, eastern Germany and Russia, vastly expanding Polish territory. He became Poland's first king in 1025, but his untimely death later that same year left Poland disunified and vulnerable to hordes of invaders and conquerors for the ensuing 300 years.

The Piast name re-emerged when the aspiring Casimir the Great assumed the throne in 1333. A clever statesman, he developed a strong national defense, promoted trade and industry, and granted extensive privileges to the Jews. Casimir was instrumental in developing a viable central government, boosting the economy, and encouraging literacy and the development of a Polish culture. Upon his death, the crown passed to Louis of Hungary by prearrangement with Casimir. Louis paid but slight attention to Poland, however, ruling Poland through regents.

Although Louis' daughter Jadwiga was elected Queen of Poland in 1384, her marriage in 1386 to Jagiello, Grand Duke of Lithuania, ceded control to him. In effect, Jagiello left both Poland and Lithuania autonomous, and Poland continued along the course set by Casimir the Great.

The Polish empire reached its peak by the 1500s. Its territory now included large parts of central Europe, Russian lands and Ukraine. Economically and politically, Poland was a major power; culturally, she had developed beyond most of her neighbors. However, following the Jagiellian era, a succession of ineffectual rulers served to weaken every aspect of Polish life, social, economic and spiritual. The debilitated and dispirited Poland fell easy prey to its aggressive neighbors, offering little resistance to a series of three separate partitions of their country, until it ceased to exist as a separate nation. The first invasion and subsequent partitioning took place in 1772, when Austria, Prussia and Russia occupied a third of the nation. Poland made a feeble attempt to recoup its losses, but the more powerful Prussian and Russian forces easily repelled the Polish forces and took a bigger bite of Polish land the following year. This second partitioning led to a Polish rebellion under the heroic leadership of Thaddeus Kosciusko, but with so many of their countrymen now under foreign rule and so little territory left to support the rebellion, the foredoomed effort failed miserably. The balance of the decimated Poland was then divided among the victors, Austria, Russia and Prussia, in 1795.

Some twenty years later, the ever-tenacious Poles once more tried to salvage their country, culture and language by joining forces with Napoleon I in his war against the Austrians and Prussians. But Napoleon's ultimate defeat in 1815 shattered this Polish dream.

World War I seems to have been the turning point in Polish history. Jozef Pilsudski, a Polish politician, led Polish forces from Austria against the Russians and, one year after the war began, Russia retreated from their occupied section of Poland. The Austrians and Germans then decided that a Polish kingdom should be established under their joint protection. Meanwhile, in Paris, another Polish politician in exile, Roman Dmowski, won support of the Allied Forces in the formation of the Polish National Committee. After the Allied victory in 1918, a Polish republic was proclaimed and Pilsudski was named its first Chief of State.

The 1919 Treaty of Versailles, under the auspices of the newly-formed League of Nations, ceded a great deal of Poland's partitioned territory back to her. She then regained her all-important access to the Baltic Sea, but when Poland demanded the return of her eastern territories, it resulted in war. The Polish forces prevailed and, under the Treaty of Riga, Russia reluctantly surrendered much of the Polish territory they had occupied.

The Treaty of Versailles, although outwardly gracious in its terms, was a great disappointment to the Jews. Although it designated Palestine the national homeland of the Jews, it failed to give them the one thing they most wanted: the full right of citizenship in their countries of residence, wherever they were currently living in Europe. Actually, the treaty worsened the plight of all European Jews. This cannot be blamed on the treaty, but on the pervading identification of Jews with Bolshevism. Unfortunately, as we touched upon in the "Bukharan Dancer" chapter, the two most prominent Bolshevik leaders, Lenin and Trotsky, denied their own Jewish roots. Trotsky, Lenin's right hand and CEO in the Bolshevik revolution, created and controlled the savage Red Army and manifested his revulsion for his fellow Jews by his ferocity towards them. Ironically, it was the Jewishness of Lenin and Trotsky, not their anti-Semitism, that was communicated and enlarged upon until the Bolshevik revolution was mistakenly identified with *all* the Jews. This ultimately led to the murder of countless thousands of innocent Jews throughout Europe, especially in Poland and Hungary after the Bolshevik invasion of those countries failed.

The Treaty of Versailles resulted in a traumatic change in the demography of Europe. In Poland, which had been partitioned into three distinct parts for more than a hundred years, reunification was a slow, painful process. The citizens of each area, each with its own ideology, were extremely resentful of being uprooted yet another time. But as the Polish leaders set about strengthening the economy and developing a uniform system of government, education and transportation, a feeling of national unity began to return. Poland was a viable, solidified nation once more. But dark clouds were looming on the horizon.

The year was 1939, and Hitler was demanding that Danzig (Gdansk) be given to Germany. When the Poles refused to surrender their only access to the Baltic Sea (which had been returned to them by the Treaty of Versailles only twenty years earlier), Hitler invaded Poland and World War II had begun.

Poland was devastated along with most of Europe. Millions of Poles were put into concentration camps during the Soviet and German occupations. Most of the 3 million Polish Jews and 3 million Christian Poles died in the shameful Holocaust. The atrocities in the camps, perpetrated against the Jews and non-Jews who tried to help them, are well documented. However, what I view as even more shocking were the events that immediately followed cessation of hostilities. The survivors of the Holocaust, left undernourished, traumatized, without homes or families and with little hope for the future, were herded into squalid relocation camps like so many stray animals. In fact, even the legendary General Patton, hailed by the world as a great liberator, callously remarked that it was impossible to think that these survivors were ever anything more than subhumans if they could be so degraded in the short span of four years. Those survivors who were returned to their countries of origin – often against their will – were further subjected to anti-Semitic riots, beatings, and deaths.

When the war ended in 1945, Germany relinquished all the territories it had taken from Poland. The Soviet Union, obviously, did not. The Poles bitterly opposed the imposition of Communist rule. But, leaderless and devastated, they were "persuaded" to submit to Stalin's horrific police power, exile, humiliation and torture.

Since our subject is Jewish, let us examine what life was like for Jews while all the above-mentioned destruction of Poland was going on.

The Jewish population in prewar Poland was the largest in Eastern Europe, numbering more than 3 million. After the debacle, this number was reduced to approximately a mere 5,000. The prewar Jews, predominantly Europeans and escapees from Spain during the Spanish Inquisition, came to Poland in

54

the belief that this was the safest place for them. These immigrants were joined by many of the Jews who were expelled from Portugal four years after the Inquisition. This was during the time that Poland flourished and enjoyed economic stability, cultural achievement, and an enlightened attitude toward the influx of so many Jews. Not only did they provide a boost to Poland's economy, but their presence increased populations in territories where they were most needed. The agrarian skills they brought with them helped expand agriculture and, subsequently, the trading industry.

In 1503, the Polish monarch made what seemed to be a magnanimous gesture toward the Jews: he appointed Jacob Polak Rabbi of Poland. This gave the Jews a certain amount of self-government. This appointment though was like a double-edged sword. By allowing the Jewish communities to prosper, Poland vastly broadened its tax base. Also, by using Jews as tax-raising agents, the government established, in effect, a buffer between the monarchy and the taxpayers. "Let the Jewish tax collectors be blamed in the event of tax hikes", seems to have been the thinking, and, indeed, reluctant taxpayers were often abusive toward the despised tax collectors. I am reminded of a photograph in Roman Vishniac's pictorial portrayal of pre-Holocaust Polish Jews; it depicts a lonely Jewish woman tax collector sitting huddled at a steel box, sheltered from the harsh climate by nothing more than an umbrella.

The rabbi, unfortunately, turned out to be less interested in the democratic ministering to the needs of his constituents than in establishing an oligarchy. He misused his position by appointing a select few cronies as "judges", and channelled the revenues he collected into financial schemes which benefited only himself and his inner circle of friends. As the Rabbi became more and more involved in communal affairs, business and finance, the more affluent Jews developed another source of income: moneylending, called credit-finance.

By 1607, Jewish communities in Poland and Lithuania began lending money to other Jews for a percentage (at interest). With this expanded line of credit, hitherto denied them, Jews were now able to engage in businesses and thus contribute greatly to the accelerating Polish economy. But as successful as Jewish businessmen seemed to be, there was a fatal flaw beneath the surface of their relationship with the Polish monarchy: Jews were not allowed to own businesses or properties. This left them in an extremely vulnerable position. They had Polish landlords, from whom they leased the land and buildings they used for agrarian purposes or as shopkeepers. The Polish aristocrats owned the land, the Germans were in charge of the seaports, and the Dutch owned the ships.

Meanwhile, Western Europe was expanding and needed to import more grain to supply its burgeoning population. The Polish aristocrats hired Jews to operate their estates and to create new wheat-growing areas in the hope of taking advantage of meeting this demand. The Jews also leased land from the aristocrats for their own purposes. They built mills and distilleries, breweries and inns on a work-for-hire arrangement with the landowners. Later, they bought river boats from the profits and were able to engage in small trade. From the major wheat producers, they bought the excess grain and, by using their small boats, traded the wheat for items they could sell in their shops.

Primarily, Jewish businesses dealt in practical, useful items, dealing directly with the peasant end users of their wares. Again, the Jews were being used as middlemen, buffering the aristocrat landowners from the peasants. Thus, when the owners raised rents, the lessees were compelled to raise the prices of their produce and goods in order to maintain a profit margin. But, since they were the only ones to have direct contact with the irate consumers, the Jews took all the blame for inflated prices. It was the classic "kick the dog" syndrome, which could only culminate in disaster. And it did.

Matters finally came to a head with a peasant uprising in 1648 led by an aristocrat, Bogdan Chmielnicki. His targets were the Polish monarchy, the Catholic Church and, especially, the Jews. The Polish landowners abandoned the Jews to save their own necks and some 100,000 were slaughtered in the ensuing pogrom.

What, to me, has always seemed dangerously naive about the Jews throughout the world is that they always clustered together in isolated communities, like ghettos. In most places it was required, but I feel they would have chosen to do so anyway. They were somewhat independent of the rest of the community for religious reasons; they had their own kosher butchers, their own schools, rabbis, and so on. But implicit in their ghetto behavior is a false sense of security they seemed to derive from having their own social and intellectual community to escape to when day was done. If I compare them with us immigrants, I find that all immigrating cultures share this clustering trait. I have often heard New York City described as "the Great Melting Pot". Actually, it was anything but that. No one melted: Greeks settled among Greeks, the Irish among Irish, the Jews among Jews and so on. At best, the pot contained an "imperfect colloid", with none of the diverse ingredients completely blending. The net effect: each culture remained essentially separate and intact. Today, through assimilation and intermarriage, these ethnic and/or religious separations are less pronounced, but, to some extent, they persist.

Returning to our subject, Abraham, allow me to try positioning him, his family and his Hassidic sect into the history of Poland and, eventually, of Palestine.

By the 18th century, more than half of the worldwide Jewish population lived in Eastern Europe. At that time and place, a religious revival was beginning. Under the leadership of a zealot named Israel ben Eliezor, Hassidism was founded. Its system of prayer differed from the time-honored practices in intensity and purpose. The hierarchy of the Hassidics combined the beliefs of the Polish Jews and the Spanish Jews, adding more literature to their prayers and incorporating much of the mysticism known as Kabbalism. They broke away from traditional Judaism and opened their own houses of prayer; they changed their way of dress to long black coats and fur-trimmed hats. Needless to say, their conspicuousness shocked the Jewish community, who were striving so hard to maintain a low profile. In spite of protests from orthodox Jews, Hassidism quickly spread all over Poland and Lithuania. It took hold in Germany and, from there, was adopted in many countries throughout the rest of the world.

Abraham's forebears embraced Hassidism in Poland in the early 19th century. They emigrated to Palestine and settled among other Hassidim in the Old City of Jerusalem in 1847. In our interview, Abraham claimed that the move to Palestine was not the result of social, political or economic pressures, but was inspired by their love for the Holy Land. He insisted that Hassidim had been coming by sea to Palestine for the same reason since the year 1765. I find these statements hard to accept, based on what we now know about the centuries-long plight of the Hassidim in Poland, especially their persecution at the hands of Elijah ben Solomon Zalman, a vengeful Orthodox Jewish leader, who in the 18th century declared Hassidism an abomination.

Between 1780 and 1850 there was a mass exodus of Polish Hassidim to Palestine, where they began building praying centers for the sole purpose of studying the Torah. But, even in the Holy Land, their black caftans, fur headdresses and, especially, their disdainful attitude toward Conservative Jews stirred up controversy.

Abraham takes a dim view of all Jews who are not Hassidic. He claims that, though the Conservatives themselves are not bad, they form a dangerous link to the less-observant Reform movement, which he deplores as being lip-service Jews caught up in secularism. He still considers these marginal Jews as part of his race, but likens their religious practices to a stage performance. "Reformism is a forgery," declares Abraham. "It takes real life and makes a theater out of it!" He quotes Shakespeare at this point, drawing an analogy: "To be or not to be ..." Abraham feels there is no midway in the religion. Either you accept the religion as the Hassidim do, or you don't accept anything.

Abraham was well versed in the history of Hassidic traditions. When I asked him about the origins and significance of the strict Hassidic code, he answered with such ready volubility that I imagine he has been asked the same question on many occasions.

The clothing originated in Europe, he says, where it was copied both from the immigrating European Jewry (the Ashkenazim), and from those who came later from Spain, Jordan, Iraq, Yemen, and so on (the Sephardim). When the first group of Ashkenazi Hassidim migrated to Palestine, they borrowed money from Palestinian Arabs to buy property. After a few years, some of this original group died and the rest left, leaving the Arabs in debt. Later, when the Sepharadi Hassidim arrived (wearing traditional Hassidic attire), the Arabs took them to be Ashkenazim and approached them for remuneration. The Sephardim finally convinced the Arabs that they were not of the same sect as the Ashkenazim and, therefore, not responsible for their debts. The Arabs, and rightfully so, began looking in earnest for the Ashkenazi Hassidim and every time they caught one they took his clothes. So, to escape discovery by the Arab creditors, the Ashkenazi Hassidim adopted the dress of the Sephardi Hassidim. The attire became traditional among the Hassidim, and thus holy.

The *talit* (a religious prayer shawl) must be worn at all times, with the *tzitzit*, or fringes, which hang from the four corners, visible. The dress code is uncompromisingly adhered to by all Hassidim; younger orthodox Jews, who also adhere to this rule, however, are beginning to be influenced by their neighbors. It is not at all uncommon to see young adults and children wearing Western-style clothing – with the *tzitzit* hanging out from under such garments as a New York Yankees sweatshirt and Levi jeans!

The traditional black topcoat, which Abraham calls a caftan, has changed but little through the years. The Ashkenazim caftan folds right over left; the

Sephardim folds in the opposite direction. The Ashkenazim adopted their fold because, claims Abraham, it was written in the Kabbalah that this would strengthen the right side over the left. There is apparently some religious significance to every minute detail of the construction of the garment, including the number of stitches, but such minutiae would contribute nothing to the enlightenment of anyone but an aspiring Hassidic seamstress, I am afraid. Abraham's grandfather had separate caftans for the beginning of the month (Rosh Hodesh), and a white one for Rosh Hashanah (the Jewish New Year) and Yom Kippur (the holiest day in the Jewish religion, the day on which all sins are atoned for and the day that it is believed one is written in the book of life). There are caftans for the Sabbath and other holidays. There are special places in Jerusalem where the caftans are made by Hassidic women. Abraham explained that the Hassidic dress code does not represent a level of religion, but more an intensity of belief. The dress is not as important as the maintenance of a tradition. He made an analogy between the Hassidim and English barristers, who maintain the ages-old tradition of wearing wigs and robes in court. This custom creates a distinct atmosphere, a special aura, as much does the wearing of a white caftan on holy days.

The most fascinating clothing item to me is the traditional hat (*shtreimel*) which Abraham is wearing in Lunda's painting. Worn only on the Sabbath and other important holy days, this beautiful headpiece originated in Europe and has been kept in its original form. Once imported from Europe, *shtreimels* are now manufactured in Israel. There are two types of fur on an authentic *shtreimel*, and both furs have to be imported; one comes from Europe and the other from the United States. Not having much knowledge of furs, I can only guess that they are fox furs. All I can verify is that one is black and the other is red. The major differences between hats made in Israel and those made in Europe are the quality and the cost, according to Abraham. To his eye, a Jerusalem-made *shtreimel*, with its broader brim, was more elegant than the European version. But, for what I suspect to be economic considerations, the Jerusalem-made *shtreimel* uses a less expensive fur.

I enjoyed this encounter with Abraham. It is probably the only time I will ever have the privilege of coming this close to a Hassidic rabbi. It gave me valuable insight into a fascinating culture, it presented Lunda with an imposing model, and it gave me a better feeling for the Hassidim than I could ever hope to get from reading about them in a book.

AUTHOR'S NOTE: For more about the Hassidim, read the "Diary" chapter, where I discuss the colorful Lag B'Omer celebration atop Mount Meron.

Samaritan, Israel—
Lunda Hoyle Gill—©
FRSA 1988

62

A SAMARITAN HIGH PRIEST

I n researching the Samaritans, I could not help thinking of that classic Japanese movie, *Rashomon*, wherein the same story is told from three viewpoints. I must admit that it was frustrating and tedious to pore through the several differing versions of the Samaritans' origins and try to arrive at the truth – and I am not sure that theologians, historians and anthropologists will ever be able to determine which version is true. So, in the interest of objectivity, I will begin with the non-sectarian (and most commonly accepted) version, then touch upon the Jewish and Samaritan interpretations later in the chapter. You will notice I differentiate between Jewish and Samaritan. That is because Orthodox Jews do not consider Samaritans to be pure Jews, and also because there are more than a few anti-Jewish arguments in the historical writings of the Samaritans.

It is generally accepted that the Samaritans are a hybrid tribe which evolved after Sargon II, the King of Assyria, conquered Samaria (the northern kingdom of Israel) in 721 BCE. He dispersed most of the defeated Samaritans (one of the ten Lost Tribes) and replaced them with Assyrians (the ancient Persians-Iranians), probably because they had no emotional ties to the land and its traditions. The Jews who remained apparently merged with these "strangers" and a new Semitic culture evolved: the Samaritans.

The southern part of the kingdom was called Judah. As you will remember from the Bukharan chapter, when Nebuchadnezzar overran Jerusalem and destroyed its temple, the conquered Judeans were exiled to Babylonia. However, no foreigners were brought in to replace this population. Unlike the Samaritans, who intermarried with the Assyrian invaders, the Judean exiles remained homogeneous. After about seventy years in Babylon, they were allowed to return to Jerusalem, led by a scribe named Ezra, to live and rebuild their razed temple and a wall surrounding the city.

By this time, the Samaritans, now grown in numbers, strength and prosperity, heard that the Jews were rebuilding the temple and offered to participate. To the dismay of the Samaritans, the offer was rejected by the Jews, who considered them to have surrendered their purity by intermarrying with their Assyrian conquerors. This rebuff triggered the indignant withdrawal of the Samaritans from any further attempts to reconcile their differences with the Judeans. In Chaim Potok's *Wanderings, A History of the Jews*, the author paints a picture of the temple incident which is more pejorative toward the Samaritans. He claims that, rather than making a conciliatory effort to help the

63

Jews, the Samaritans harassed them and effectively prevented the reconstruction project for several years. It was only after Ezra returned from Babylon with the incontrovertible power of Persian law backing him that the Samaritans desisted and the temple was rebuilt without further interruption from the northern kingdom adversaries.

The Samaritans returned to their own holy place on Mount Gerizim and around 333 BCE established their own community. They built their temple there and proclaimed themselves the only true successors of Ancient Israel.

Their sacred book is the Samaritan Pentateuch (the five books of Moses). Their religion is monotheistic (they believe in one God) and they are extremely ethical in their observance of their liturgy. Interestingly, the Samaritans do not call themselves Samaritans, but rather *Shomronim* (guardians) of the Torah, as do the Jews. Although both faiths use the Old Testament as the basis for their beliefs, the Jewish version has been modified by the Samaritans. They reference their history in three basic works: the Tolidah (the Chain of Priests, from Creation to the present); the Samaritan Book of Joshua, and Annals of Abu'l Fath. The author of the last of these was commissioned by the High Priest Phineas to write this "official history" of the Samaritans, but many scholars are convinced the resultant tome is riddled with inaccuracies. There is also a Samaritan Arabic Joshua and Samaritan Hebrew Joshua. No doubt these versions exist because of the Samaritan language dichotomy: those who live in Nablus (ancient Shechem) speak Arabic; those who live in Holon speak Hebrew.

Except for when they are wearing their ceremonial robes and scarves, the Holon Samaritans are indistinguishable from their Jewish fellow citizens. The same can be said about the Nablus Samaritans, who seem to mingle peaceably with their Arabic neighbors.

According to a pamphlet written by the current High Priest of the Samaritans, Yusef Abu Al Hassan Cohen, the Samaritans trace their origin back to Moses. They believe themselves to be descendants of the tribes of Ephraim, Levi and Manasseh. They base these beliefs on a version of the five books of Moses (a Torah) they claim to have found on Mount Gerizim, which the Samaritans consider to be the holiest of holy places and the center of the universe. Written in ancient Hebrew on goatskin, it is said to date from around 3606 BCE, about thirteen years after the death of Moses. Since the Jewish Torah was written in Aramaic script, but much later, around 622 BCE, and not in its present form, the Samaritan Pentateuch, if authenticated, would antedate the Jewish

Torah by many years and substantiate the Samaritan claims, which derive from Deuteronomy 11:29 and 27:12.

Samaritan literature contends that all ancient Israelites were unified politically and religiously until Eli, a leader of the tribe of Levi, divided the nation of the Judeans into two sections (for some obscure reason). The north section was ruled by the Priest Aza, while Eli ruled over the south.

This schism resulted in bitter enmity between the two factions. When border clashes widened the breach, Eli joined forces with "foreign antagonists" and declared war on the north. Overwhelmed by the invading horde, the northerners were vanquished and exiled to Assyria, thus reducing the number of Samaritans remaining in Israel to a mere handful.

The history of this era, as recounted in chapter seventeen of the Second Book of Kings, is rejected by the Samaritans, as I would expect. In this version they are presented as heathens who, even when given a chance to atone for their anti-God practices, rejected the offering and continued to do evil. In those writings, however, the Samaritans are portrayed as descendants of the northern kingdom of Israel, who were exiled around 721 BCE. I have been led to understand from some of the people I interviewed that although the Samaritans have rejected this chapter, they have used Saint Luke's chapter ten, which depicts them as we commonly refer to them, the "Good Samaritan". I chose the word used due to their presence at the Vatican, citing this chapter as a means of receiving monies to help restore their community. In any case, because they supposedly intermarried with strangers in the Diaspora, and perhaps because of what was recanted in chapter seventeen, when they returned to Israel from exile, they were considered impure by the southern group of Jews, who had returned from Babylon, and forbidden from participating in the reconstruction of the temple in Jerusalem. They themselves state that a Samaritan man can marry any woman as long as she converts to Samaritanism.

The Jewish interpretation of Samaritan history agrees with the Book of Kings version in respect to the matter of paganism. Where the Jewish teachings differ from the others is in the genealogy of the Samaritans. In Jewish lore, the self-proclaimed Samaritans were never what they claimed to be; instead, they were actually Kootim (from a territory between Assyria and Mesopotamia called Koot). These relocated Assyrians were brought into northern Judea as replacements for the Jews who were either slain or deported to Babylon. This implies that no Jews were allowed to remain in Israel and those Kootim who asked to participate in the rebuilding of the temple in Jerusalem were declared (by the Jewish leader Nehemia) non-Jewish impostors. Even today, the Jews refer to Samaritans as Kootim. So the more one reads and hears, the more one wonders just who and what are the Samaritans. In the absence of incontrovertible evidence to support either side of the argument, I refer you to *The Book of Jewish Knowledge* by Nathan Ausubel, published in 1964 by Crown Publishers, New York. He hypothesizes that: "The Samaritans were not so much a dissident sect in Judaism as a tragic accident of history." The author is disinclined to label the Samaritans "Kootim", and attributes the Jewish-Samaritan problem not only to the action taken by Zerubabel (the Jewish leader who began the rebuilding the temple on Mount Zion), when he humiliated the Samaritans by rejecting them as brother-Jews, but to the later (circa 458) actions of Ezra and Nehemiah in declaring all marriages that had been contracted with Samaritans to be invalid. Ezra, the most uncompromising of the Jewish leaders, "proceeded to take even harsher measures: He drove out of the congregation of Israel all those who had intermarried with Samaritans or were the seed of such a union, and, in addition, barred them from all religious and social intercourse with other Jews."

So there you have the three conflicting histories of the Samaritans. It is not incumbent upon me to judge the validity of any one of them. Unless and until the Samaritans submit their "original and authentic" Torah for the sort of intensive scientific analysis the Shroud of Turin has been undergoing for years, its validity will remain undetermined. Apparently, the suspicious Samaritan hierarchy, realizing they have nothing to gain and everything to lose by allowing their sacrosanct relic to be taken from its Ark and scrutinized by non-believers, remain deaf to such a suggestion.

The strikingly handsome gentleman in Lunda's painting is the High Priest Yusef Al-Hassan Cohen. His very name suggests the probability of some Arab-Jewish intermarriage between his forebears. By a stroke of good fortune, our meeting with this most powerful Samaritan leader took place on Mount Gerizim during the holiday of Passover. (The story of our serendipitous encounter is to be found later in the chapter.)

As commanded in their Torah, the Samaritans must assemble atop Mount Gerizim to pray before the ark on three different holy days each year. A couple of days before the Samaritan Passover (the holiday celebrating the Jews' exodus from Egypt), we learned that only a few hundred invitations had been issued to the thousands of non-Samaritans wishing to attend the colorful Samaritan Passover rites. Elisha and I telephoned everyone we knew who might have enough influence to wangle admission for us, but our efforts were fruitless. I was heartsick. I knew that this would be one of the few times that non-believers are permitted to witness all but the most sacrosanct temple functions of this Samaritan holy day, and it seemed certain that we were going to miss it. But our resourceful guide, Dantchu, came to our rescue at the eleventh hour. Somehow, through a friend of a friend, he obtained special invitations – and won my eternal gratitude.

With Dantchu leading the way, we "caravaned" to the top of Mount Gerizim, parked the cars and strolled down into the village. I later learned that the many small houses were the second homes of the Samaritans, occupied only in the summer and on holy days.

We quickly found two Samaritan subjects for Lunda to sketch; the first man was a retired civil-service worker. While Lunda was sketching him, a distinguished-looking gentleman approached and, after watching her at work, invited us to come to his house and paint him. When Lunda finished sketching her first subject, we walked in the direction the intended second subject had indicated and entered what we took to be his home. But, unwittingly, we found ourselves in the wrong house! This was the house of the High Priest, who, providently, welcomed us and graciously agreed to be the subject of this chapter. But, because he was scheduled to lead his followers in prayer within the hour, he could not grant me much time. Elisha helped Lunda prepare her palette and, although the High Priest was fluent in English, I decided to save most of my questions for his accommodating daughter-in-law and give the time-pressured Lunda a chance to sketch undisturbed.

Nawal Cohen is married to the High Priest's eldest son, a moneychanger in Nablus (he exchanges dollars for Israeli shekels and Jordanian dinar). Nawal is employed by the police department of Nablus and speaks Hebrew and Arabic. Much of the information that follows was derived from my interview with this knowledgeable young lady.

At the end of our brief but productive session with the High Priest and his daughter-in-law, we expressed our gratitude and headed for the nearby sacred ground where the ritualistic slaughter of the rams was to take place. Elisha and I sat on wooden bleachers amid hundreds of other spectators, listened to the singing of the Haggadah (the book used to describe the Jews' exodus from Egypt), and then watched (with some squeamishness, I confess) the ceremonial sacrifice. I left the actual eyeballing of the grisly spectacle to Elisha, while I read the pamphlet (written in fractured English), which told me all I had to know about the ritual of the rams:

Every Passover, each Samaritan family brings a "perfect" ram (meaning a healthy animal with no physical defects) to the same designated arena atop Mount Gerizim. There the ram (one to each family) is ritualistically slaughtered by the men of the family, skinned, skewered on a stout pole and buried in a pit of hot wood to bake for a designated number of hours. Any non-kosher (unclean) parts are immediately burned on a pile of oak branches. After the cooked ram is unearthed, the family takes its ram home and eats as much as each member wants. However, in remembrance of the haste with which the Jews fled Egypt, the meal must be eaten hastily. No guests are permitted to eat with the family, and the meal consists only of the baked ram and home-baked matzo (unleavened bread). Whatever food remains is burned.

This particular year, the holiday fell on a Friday, which meant that they had to wait until after the Sabbath to burn the remains. The Jews, who abandoned the practice of sacrificing animals after the destruction of the last temple in 70 CE, observe Passover in their homes, ritually. Instead of a public sacrifice, they have a Passover meal, read the Haggadah during the meal and use symbols of the hardships experienced during the Exodus which have been placed on a Seder (order) plate. The Seder plate is divided into six sections. The biblical reference in the Old Testament, Numbers 9:11, uses the plural form of bitter herbs, so at least two are used on this night. The first bitter herb is called *Maror*, usually in the form of horseradish, and meant to signify the harsh and bitter life of the Jews during their enslavement in Egypt. *Hazeret* is another bitter herb, the second on the plate, and can be one of many as long as it is bitter, such as a radish. The third section contains a vegetable of some sort like parsley, which is dipped in salt water before being sampled. The reason for this is unknown to me, but according to *The Jewish Book of Why* by Alfred J. Kolatch, this custom dates back to the 1st and 2nd century in Jerusalem, where a vegetable was used as the first course of a formal meal. *Haroset* is a combination of chopped walnuts, apples, red wine and dates, or some variation of that, meant to represent the mortar bricks the Jews had to make and use for construction for their Egyptian masters. A roasted shank bone has a double meaning. Not only does it represent the paschal lamb ceremony that the Samaritans actually perform, but it is also symbolic of the long arm of God. The last item on the plate is a roasted egg. I have been told by my own elders that the roasted egg is to remind us of the twice-destroyed temple in Jerusalem.

There are many other differences between Samaritans and Jews. For instance, while interviewing the High Priest, I noticed that his *talit* (prayer shawl) was fringed quite differently than the Jewish shawl. There was no particular religious significance to the fringe-work, which is a detail of liturgically-mandated exactness on the *talit* of a Jew. The Old Testament reference for the *tzitzit* (fringes) can be found in Numbers 15:37-41. The fringes are more important than the garment in following this commandment. In fact, there is no commandment for a prayer shawl, but where else would you hang the fringes? The fringes are to be hung from the four corners of a garment and in the same biblical reference it commands that they be seen, therefore worn outside. When I questioned the High Priest about the absence of these corner fringes on his shawl, he shrugged and replied that such laws are observed spiritually rather than literally. Since he is the absolute leader in matters of Samaritan prayer and liturgical interpretation, I project his answer to suggest that there may have been myriad reforms in the formularies of Samaritan doctrine through the centuries. These deviations from their root beliefs I leave for some student of comparative religion to research as a thesis for a Master's degree.

Another major difference between the Samaritans and Jews in Israel is the manner in which they bury their dead. The Samaritans use coffins, while the Jews are forbidden to do so. The latter inter the deceased wrapped in a shroud. This is in keeping with the biblical "ashes to ashes, dust to dust" axiom. I specify in Israel, as Jews anywhere else are buried in coffins. I suspect that is because they are not in the Holy Land so their souls must go back.

The shroud is an interesting item. Before the destruction of the second temple in 70 CE, the material of the traditional burial shroud of the Jews was very ostentatious and did not depend on the financial situation of the family, but rather on show. Many Jews were buried under shrouds, the likes of which they were never able to afford in their lifetimes. After the destruction of the second temple, the Patriarch Rabban Gamaliel II issued a rabbinical decree forbidding this ostentation. Thereafter, the requirement was that every Jew, regardless of his financial or social position, be buried in exactly the same way. The shroud was to be made of an inexpensive, unadorned linen cloth. This shroud is called *tachrichim* in Hebrew. The Samaritans burn candles at the head and feet of the corpse and end their mourning period by the following Sabbath. They, like the Jews, do not bury their dead on the Sabbath, but as soon thereafter as possible. Following the burial, the Jews sit *shiva* (the number seven) for seven days at home. There they receive family and friends offering condolences and bringing food to the mourner(s). The way I was raised, all mirrors in the home were covered, no mourner greeted a guest, simply acknowledged their presence by a shake of the head, sat on wooden boxes and never got up to prepare food for guests. On the contrary, that was the reason guests brought food. It is also during this mourning period that it is appropriate to bring sweets, so the mourners can ingest something sweet to take away their bitterness.

After the seven days of mourning, the mourners then get up and are then able to take care of other matters they may have neglected. However, on the thirtieth day after death, a stone is unveiled in the cemetery, and it is customary to return to the grave site for that ceremony. Upon the death of a parent, as I observed, even among many non-observant Jewish men, no razor is used on the head. They do not shave or have haircuts for the thirty-day period. Most Jews still practice the ancient tradition of tearing their clothes to signify mourning the death of a relative or loved one. It is not uncommon for Jews not to participate in any social functions for one year following the death. But much of that is up to the individual and the depth of his or her belief.

Most Samaritans either make their own clothing or have it made by tailors or seamstresses. They rarely, if ever buy ready-to-wear clothes from shops. An educated guess on my part would be that it is more economical to have something made than to buy it in a shop. However, this practice is not observed by many of the younger Samaritans, especially since the introduction of television and the resultant exposure to European and American programs and commercials.

When you consider that the Samaritan community consists of a mere 550-odd persons (they include the fetuses of pregnant women in their tally), and they all live in either Holon or Nablus, it is understandable that they share a strong sense of family. Although their ancestors were decimated (or exiled) by the Assyrians nearly 2,700 years ago, and at one time were reduced in number to less than 200, I was curious as to why they had regenerated so slowly. Nawal Cohen's explanation: Samaritan women are forbidden to marry outside their faith (although the men may marry a non-Samaritan woman if she converts and undergoes purification rites). From other sources, I gathered that, just as experienced by the Circassians, inbreeding among the Samaritans has resulted in a disproportionate number of miscarriages and birth defects. By implication, this would seem to indicate that young Samaritan couples of the same bloodline would be somewhat in trepidation about having children.

Samaritan wedding ceremonies are festive occasions when both communities gather for the celebrations. So many of the residents of both communities are somehow related that it is inevitable for them to participate. Currently, they are not held in special facilities, but there are plans for the creation of a wedding chapel on Mount Gerizim. The festivities begin on the Saturday evening preceding the nuptial rites, which are performed on the following Tuesday. The male celebrants alternately chant from the Scriptures and feast (depending upon how much money the groom's family can afford to spend). The evenings are devoted to dancing: the group from Holon performs Hebrew dances; those from Nablus dance Arabic style. A day before the wedding vows are exchanged, the future bride's family hosts a henna party, which is an elaborate predecessor of the modern American bridal shower. However, the word henna is merely symbolic and derives from the traditional henna ceremony of the Yemenites, as well as many other groups. You will read a detailed description of this ancient custom in the Yemenite chapter. During the party, the bride-to-be wears a dress of pink, red or any bright color. But she wears only white (signifying purity) on her wedding day. On the Friday following the exchanging of vows, the newlyweds return to the home of the bride's parents. Saturday morning is spent indoors, praying. The balance of the day, they celebrate by feasting, chanting and receiving their well-wishing friends.

If someone asked me for a prognosis on the future of the Samaritans, I would predict a very positive one. They are considered a separate religious sect within the land of Israel, and freely practice their beliefs and customs.

I recall when I began research on this group I thought of them as a small and fragile community. When the research was as complete as possible, I realized that throughout history from biblical times, masses of them have been murdered or exiled reducing their numbers to very few individuals. Yet, they are still here. Their number of 550 people is still small but slowly growing.

Although this chapter was the most tedious, it was the most rewarding. It forced me to learn more about biblical history, Old and New testaments and the Samaritans. I have no regrets about the effort, and a great deal of respect for the Samaritans.

74

A YEMENITE BRIDE

As mentioned in the introduction, the term Diaspora refers to those descendants of Abraham not living in the land of Israel. The story of the Diaspora began when the Romans destroyed Jerusalem in 70 CE, and scattered the vast majority of Jews throughout Europe and Asia. Those who relocated within the Moslem countries of the Near or Middle East are called Eastern or Oriental Jews. Even though much of the Diaspora has returned to the Holy Land since 1948, many enclaves of Oriental Jews remain in such countries as Syria, Lebanon, Yemen, Iraq and Iran. In North Africa, thousands of Jews remain in Morocco, Tunisia, Ethiopia, Egypt and Sudan.

To my knowledge, no reliable research sources exist regarding the first settlements of Jews in Yemen. But an educated guess would place the earliest emigration from Palestine at the time of the Hellenistic occupation in the 2nd century CE. The best evidence of this is in the craftsmanship the Jews brought with them. Their skillful weaving, embroidery and jewelry fabrication reveal a Hellenistic influence and are considered the most significant contribution the Jews made to the arts and crafts of the Arab-Moslem culture.

As long as Jews lived in Yemen, their cultural pocket remained intact. Unlike other Jews in the Diaspora, the Yemenite Jews were culturally unique and maintained their unique identity by not intermarrying, by following all the laws of the Jewish religion and by transferring all their ancient customs, ceremonies and traditions to their children.

For centuries, Yemenite Jews endured social isolation and degradation from their unrelentingly anti-Jewish Moslem hosts. They were restricted to menial jobs; they weren't allowed to own land; the only means of transportation allowed them was mules; and most of them lived in abject poverty.

Yet the Jews clung to Judaism even in the face of persecution, compulsory conversion and death. Their unshakable faith was all that sustained them as they dreamed of the day they could return to the Holy Land.

To ensure the propagation of their religion, the most significant bonding ritual was marriage within their own infrastructure. For both Moslems and Jews, a betrothal and subsequent marriage was a week-long succession of festivities, rituals and parties sponsored by the families of the bride and groom. In many secular aspects of these occasions, the Jews adopted Moslem Yemenite customs. For example, the extremely ornate bridal raiment and the henna ceremony (which will be detailed later in the chapter) are derivative of ancient Yemenite traditions. Even among those Yemenite Jews who managed to return to Israel, these colorful practices continued. Yemenite weddings were such major events, emotionally, spiritually and financially, they most often were (and are) considered the principal form of entertainment among the community.

In 1925, an edict was passed in Yemen to force minor Jewish orphans to become Islamized. Since no one could predict whether one's children would become orphans – and since maturity was based on marital status alone – the Jews decided to safeguard their offspring's religious heritage by arranging intrafaith marriages for daughters as young as eight years of age and sons as young as eleven.

In my opinion, forced conversion to Islam was the principal, if not the only, motivating factor in the flood of emigrations by Yemenite Jews to Israel in the 20th century.

Prior to the 1925 edict of forced conversion in Yemen, when a young man reached the age of eighteen his mother and sisters would begin to look for suitable bridal prospects. The young man would be presented with more than one eligible young woman from which to choose. The choice made, it was then the obligation of the boy's father to arrange the details of the engagement. The bride's "price" was negotiated between the two families. Generally, this fee was in the form of clothing and/or jewelry. This was because Yemenite Jewish women did not work outside the home; the man was the wage-earner and a new bride needed a basic trousseau and accessories. It was the groom's responsibility to bear the cost of such essentials. Of course, in the new Israel, the post-1948 generations are more Westernized and most young Yemenite women have entered the work force. So the often exorbitant costs of the wedding generally are shared by the two families plus relatives and friends.

A patrilocal residence pattern existed in Yemen (the new bride went to live with the family of the groom), and there was a ritualistic duty performed on that occasion, wherein the bride's family implored the groom to ensure that their daughter would not suffer any abuses from her new mother-in-law or any other members of the groom's family.

Once the wedding date was decided upon by the groom's parents, massive preparations began for both families. The bride's parents prepared their daughter's dowry; the groom's parents prepared the traditional clothing and jewelry for the bride and arranged all the details of the wedding. It is interesting to note that, despite the enormous expense of the wedding and the prenuptial preparations, polygamy was a common practice of Jew and Arab alike.

Since the vast majority of Yemenite Jews were poor or lower middle class, the inordinate expenses of their elaborate weddings imposed a crushing financial burden upon the family of the groom. Generally, the groom found himself heavily in debt by the time the wedding was over. Because of this, it became the custom for the groom to take a loan from one or more friends in the close-knit Jewish community. To save the young man from the embarrassment of asking for money, the nuptial loan was taken by every groom, even by those who did not need it.

On the Sabbath preceding the wedding ceremony, the seven feast days were inaugurated. On this day, the families of the bride and groom gathered for a festive meal. Later, friends arrived to partake of the specially prepared foods, talk, and sing songs from a religious song-book called the Diwan. The Diwan is a treasury of poetry set to music by Rabbi Shalom Shabazi in the 17th century. It is used on the Sabbath, at festivals, weddings and most other social occasions.

The days preceding the wedding were devoted to seemingly interminable feasting and the ritualistic preparing and decorating of the bride and groom. On the Saturday evening preceding the wedding, all the future bride's female relatives and friends gathered in her home to dress her and lead her to a special place for the enactment of the ancient henna ceremony. This evening was called the Tatrufa night, which specifically meant the dyeing of the bride's fingertips and finger joints with henna*. Two women were designated by the

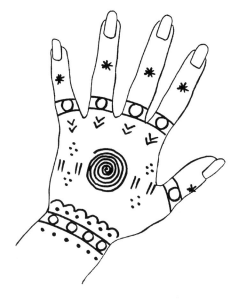

---

*Henna is derived from the leaves of the Lawsonia tree or shrub (*Lawsonia inermis alba*). Its flowers are white and yellow and have a pleasant fragrance. The plant seems to have originated in India and spread to Africa and Asia Minor. Henna may have reached Palestine via Egypt during the period of the First Temple. A tropical tree (or shrub), it flourishes today in Israel along the Jordan Valley, in En Gedi and Jericho. Henna was originally used as a base for perfume or, in its oily form, as a body dye. Even today, henna extracts are used for cosmetic and medicinal purposes. The Arabs use henna for dyeing fabrics and leather as well as their bodies. Great healing powers have been attributed to the product, and it is often found in shampoos in the belief that its chemical composition aids in the tightening of the pores of the scalp, thus preventing hair loss. In the Western world, henna is most commonly used as a reddening agent in hair dye. Its red-brown color results from the natural oxidation of the

bride's family to go from house to house inviting the females to attend. No men were allowed to be present. Two professional female singers were hired to perform a liturgy of moralistic songs which alternately thanked and praised God, asked for His blessing of the couple, prayed for divine guidance in their future life and preached to the bride to lead a decent life. Other songs were nostalgic reminiscences of childhood, instructions regarding the impending separation of the bride from her family and the bittersweet transition into this new and unknown phase of her life, marriage.

Although in recent years the henna painting is primarily for ornamental effect, the ancient practice has its roots in pagan superstition called "evil eye", or "evil spirits". Before monotheism, man considered the gods and spirits their adversaries, so envious of man's joys and triumphs that they would try to destroy him. Just as hope is the companion to man in adversity, so is fear his companion in times of good fortune – fear that it may be taken away.

Throughout a traditional henna ceremony, still done in the land of Israel, friends and family sing to the bride and dance for her. The professional singers perform a repertoire of songs which have been learned by rote. Never written down, these ancient incantations have been handed down from one generation of professionals to the next. Other songs are extemporaneous in form, much like the Afro-Cuban calypso improvisations one hears in the West Indies. Ululations (which can best be described as a kind of yodeling wail produced by oscillating the tongue behind the lips) are interspersed between songs to express happiness about the bride's impending marriage and against the evil spirits. The singing is performed a cappella (without musical accompaniment), except for two rhythm instruments peculiar to the Tatrufa. One of the

leaves after they are picked. Once dried, the leaves are ground to a powder. When henna is to be applied to a bride's hands and feet, the powder is made into a thin paste by mixing it with rosewater. On the Tatrufa night, the henna paste was rubbed onto the bride's palms, the soles of her feet, her fingertips and her nails. A female specialist was brought in to draw some very elaborate geometric designs on the feet and hands. Although I have never seen these drawings done, except in photographs, I am including in these pages a personal rendition of what they may have looked like. These areas were then wrapped in cloth and allowed to dry overnight. When the wrappings were removed in the morning, the paste was scraped off and the dyed areas now had a red-brown color.

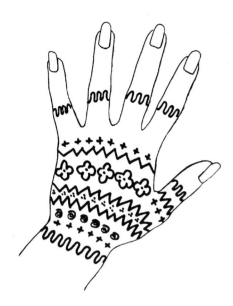

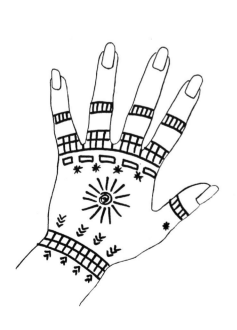

professionals plays a drum (called an *eros*), which she holds in her left hand and taps with the fingers of her right hand. The *eros* resemble a large sieve with rounded walls. The open end is covered with a taut, thin membrane (probably a piece of sheepskin) such as found on a bongo or conga drum. This membrane is called *daf* (in Hebrew, a page of paper). The drummer can produce an approximate octave of tones on the *daf* by drumming on different areas of it. The closer to the rim, the higher the tone. The second professional beats a brass cymbal (like a brass tray), called the *tzachan*, with a key. The songs are generally verse-chorus compositions, with the rhythmical accompaniment and dancing stopping for each verse, then resuming for each chorus. Throughout the Tatrufa, a special drink of *agish* (made from peels of coffee beans mixed with ginger) is served to complement the cakes and sweets (symbolizing joy) served to the guests. I have witnessed several henna ceremonies in Israel. The only difference I have noticed is in the types of food presented. I assume the difference is a question of economics. The more affluent the couple's families, the more extravagant the array of food.

In Yemen, the bride's final adornment ceremony involved shaving a corner of her hair from her forehead. The shaving was called *tadhafa*, and it served two purposes: to show that the girl is to be married, and to remind the bride of all the obligations of being a good wife. From this moment, the bride is forbidden to show her hair in public and is expected to cover her head with a scarf until after the wedding.

Traditionally, the groom was also decorated with henna and shaved. On one of seven prenuptial evenings, guests were invited to dinner at the groom's parent's home. Included among the guests was a rabbi. This practice is no longer observed in Israel, but on rare occasions a groom will dress in traditional garb and, if he chooses, will also put some henna on his palms.

In Yemen, after dinner, everyone would sing and bless the bridal couple. The groom's father was responsible for providing the henna, but the mother had the honor of coloring her son's legs. The tradition of henna coloring for the groom stems from the belief that henna applications impart strength to the muscles.

On another evening, the ceremonial shaving of the groom took place. To the accompaniment of much singing and merriment, one of the best men poured rosewater over the groom's head, then shaved off most of his hair, leaving only *payot* (hairlocks in the sideburns area).

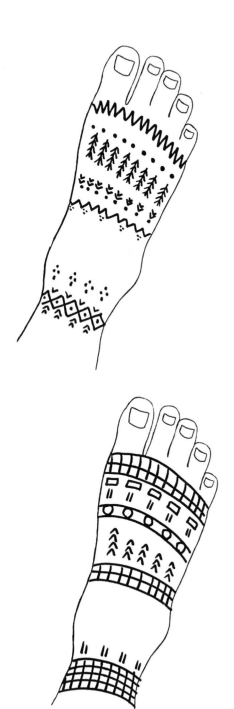

The bridal gown is extremely elaborate and beautiful. Unfortunately, it is also quite costly and cumbersome. In earlier times, in Yemen, each wedding dress was custom-made. But in modern Israel they are rented from a few enterprising women who brought the gowns and adornments from Yemen.

The sometimes-pointed headpiece is embroidered in silver and gold. From its point, down the sides of the headpiece to the shoulders, is a chain of red and white carnations resting atop *shadab* leaves. These leaves are supposed to bring good luck. Around the bride's neck are several ropes of silver beads, coins and semiprecious stones. The dress is embroidered in gold and reaches almost to the floor. To avoid exposing the bride's ankles, which is forbidden, trousers are worn under the dress and are also embroidered around the leg bottoms. A veil made of floral-patterned gold voile is hung from the crown and cascades down the back of the dress. Each arm of the bride is adorned with many gold bracelets; on every finger she wears at least one ring.

Because of the difficult life of the Yemenite woman, there was probably no other time in her life when she could expect to be this beautiful or this happy.

The beautiful Yemenite bride who posed for Lunda's painting is Ilana Said. Her parents were born in Sana, Yemen. They emigrated in 1949 via Israel's Operation Magic Carpet, which airlifted almost all of Yemen's 50,000 Jews to Israel between 1949 and 1950. Ilana, one of eight children, was born in Rechovot on September 30, 1958. Her father, who worked as a jeweler in Yemen, was trained to be a construction worker by the Solel Boneh company (a company of the Labor Federation). After twenty-five years of developing skills in this field, he was hired by the Israeli army as a construction supervisor. Seeking a larger home that was closer to his work, the family moved to the town of Ramla, where Ilana grew up, went to school and eventually graduated from a secretarial college. She presently works at her profession for the Histadrut (Labor Federation).

Although Ilana's mother and father do not approve of the increasingly evident secularism of their children's generation, the Said family has remained a close-knit unit, still observant of their religious obligations and proud of such cultural traditions as the ancient wedding rituals.

However, as is the case with every relocated culture caught up in the absorption process, the original immigrants from Yemen have undergone major changes in their lifestyle. They have had to learn a new language, Hebrew, and they have had to learn new skills when their former skills were found to be unmarketable. But despite the economic and emotional hardships these problems presented, they have prevailed, obviously preferring their acceptance in Israel to the persecution they endured in Yemen.

The children of the Yemenite immigrants, born in Israel, have had no problem assimilating into a Western-oriented society. But, except in families such as the Saids, the children, succumbing to peer pressure, were ashamed of their parents' somewhat ancient ways of dress and the often-demeaning occupations they were able to find.

Apparently, the dominating influence among immigrant cultures is Eastern European. Their Westernized fashion styles are emulated by the younger Yemenites, and their competitive materialism has made secular interests more important than religious observances.

Thus, the unique and colorful customs have given way to the customs of a dominating ethnic group. This is particularly apparent in regard to the customs of marriage. In Israel, for the most part, they have stopped shaving heads and leaving only *payot*; the bride-price was at first greatly reduced and then finally eliminated, and the henna ceremony is a token vestige of the still-festive seven days of prenuptial celebration. As the Yemenite children intermarry with Jews from other ethnic origins, fewer of them even bother with the Yemenite ceremonies.

When still observed, the henna ceremony consists of the mere painting of one fingernail, and sometimes the palms. Professional singers are generally hired, but men are now allowed to be present.

It can therefore be seen that, with the passage of time, even this remnant of a rich and elaborate ceremony will vanish.

In another generation, the Yemenite Jews will probably have lost their singularity. They will have entered and been absorbed by the culture of modern Israel, with its focus on secular Western traditions. The first generation of Yemenites, who immigrated in 1949 and 1950, remain religious, but their children are less observant, and it must be assumed that their children's children will be even less so.

The causative factors, which, in hindsight, should have been predictable, are demographic and economic changes and the influences of the dominant society.

Israel
Christian
Lunda
Hoyle
Hill © FASA 1989.

A SYRIAN ORTHODOX ARCHBISHOP

The first Syrian Orthodox Christian Church was organized in Constantinople (Turkey) during the first half of the 12th century BCE. The establishment of this church was followed by divisions in beliefs. The first two divisions began in the beginning of the 4th century BCE. One split was the Aryans, of which there are none any longer. These people were mostly among German tribes in Europe. The second division as Assyrian (the only Christian sect with no representation in Israel). These people were mostly East Asians.

The argument which produced these rifts was the result of an ecumenical council meeting held in a town called Harcarcadon in Asia Minor in 451 BCE. At that time they discussed whether Jesus had one nature or two, or a combination – divine and/or human. This belief is called Monophysitism. Although I stated that these divisions were theological, I believe they were more political. The center of Christianity at that time was in Constantinople, but the Byzantine or Roman empire dominated all Christians. Local national churches wanted more autonomy and freedom so took advantage of the controversy. After splitting from the main Church they became four Orthodox sects, the Copts, Armenians, Ethiopians and Syrians. Under the Byzantine empire, the Syrians were persecuted by other Orthodox Christians who labelled them heretics and almost destroyed them. As a result of this persecution, the Syrian Orthodox scattered to isolated and rugged mountain areas of Turkey, on the border of Kurdistan, and to Syria, then under Ottoman (Turkish) rule. Of those that remained in Byzantine Christian areas, relief from persecution only came after 700 CE when the Arabs invaded and conquered the Byzantines. The Syrian Orthodox and other persecuted Christians supported the Arabs in their quest, and because the Orthodox Christians were the enemies of the other Christians, they were considered friends of the Moslems. They were rewarded by being allowed to build churches in Armenia, Syria, Iraq and Egypt.

The largest numbers of Syrian Orthodox came to Jerusalem in the year 1100. When the Crusaders came to Jerusalem they found the local Christians and the Orthodox Armenians, Copts and Syrians living in the Old City of Jerusalem, now the Moslem quarter. Over time, many of the Syrians have left. A large group went to India, where they are called St Thomas Christians (St Thomas was one of the Apostles, and went to India). Many missionaries joined the St Thomas Christians and have been very successful. There are perhaps 1.5 million Syrian Orthodox today in India.

During World War I, a genocide was perpetrated against the Syrian Orthodox and the Armenians. The Armenian genocide has been well documented, the Syrian less. The reason is probably that they were fewer in number, less killed compared to the Armenians and also less known than they. Many refugees fled to Europe and to the United States.

The Syrian Orthodox are called Jacobites, from the reorganizer of the Church, Jacob Baradai. The Jacobites follow the Patriarchate of Antioch. According to Archbishop Dionysius Behnam Jajjawi, in 1988, the Archbishop in Jerusalem, the liturgical (religious) language is Syriac. Syriac is a branch of the Aramaic family of languages. The vernacular (other language used in daily life) would depend on where you were in the world. The Archbishop in Jerusalem explained that his language is that of Jesus and His mother – Aramaic/Syriac – and also, during prayers, Arabic. He insists that his parishioners understand the service. When I spoke to the Most Reverend Father Neno, of St Mark's Church in New Jersey, he told me he uses Syriac in their services and English outside the church.

Archbishop Jajjawi claims that his very presence in Israel represents the symbolic Church of Christianity. His diocese (the people he leads) consists of 400 families living in Bethlehem, 100 in Jerusalem and 200 in Jordan. He was appointed to Jerusalem on June 19, 1983. It was his fifth time in Israel. The first time was about thirty-five years ago when he became a priest in St Mark's Church. In 1954, in Jerusalem, he spent four years as secretary of the Convent of St Mark's Church. By 1958 he left for Lebanon to become an archbishop and spent six years as an archbishop there. At the end of the six years, he came to the United States to study for one year at the Union Theological Seminary in New York. By 1964 he returned to Damascus and spent the next six years in Syria. Before coming to Israel as archbishop, he returned to Iraq, his birthplace, to serve for two and a half years in St Matthew's Monastery.

I found Archbishop Jajjawi a delightful, insightful and intelligent man. While sitting in the courtyard sipping Cokes on this beautiful day, we spoke about how he sees the future of his religion in the land of Israel. There was a curious aura about him at that moment. The sparkle that one could only see through his eyes was suddenly glossed over. It was as if he was remembering the history of his faith and all the bitterness that came with believing. He related that he regretted losing a major portion of his parishioners after 1948, but he remained optimistic about the future of his religion in Israel. In fact, he was extremely anxious to explain the religion and share his beliefs and sentiments with me. His greatest disappointment seemed to be the dispersion of his flock, as noted before, and the greatly reduced numbers of families remaining in the Middle East. From what was a flourishing community, the remaining occupants of the monastery are the archbishop and two monks. The archbishop remains spirited and hopeful. He is making every effort to keep whatever of his flock remains in close contact with each other. They have a youth club and plans to open a school for their children to learn their language and writing. The community is organized around the church and the monastery. Archbishop Jajjawi explained the two types of writing they use. The older is Estraglinion, and it is in this script that their holy books are written. They have no printing presses in Jerusalem for this script, so holy books are reprinted by hand. There are a handful of monks who still know how to do this. One of them, Father Simon, lives in the monastery in Jerusalem. The archbishop says he is also familiar with this ancient script. The new writing is called Strato, and for this they now have printing presses.

The mainstay of support of the Syrian Orthodox community is as antique and art dealers. They also have a souvenir industry, catering for the most part to pilgrimages, and they work primarily with items they make from mother-of-pearl and olive wood.

The Syrian Orthodox have another claim to fame. A Bedouin in the desert was searching for a goat which had gone astray. He looked all over for this obstinate goat and thought he might have wandered into a nearby cave. With that in mind, the Bedouin entered the cave. He did not find his goat, but he found something very curious. Since he could not read, he collected his find and brought it to Archbishop Athansius Y. Samuel, a predecessor of Archbishop Jajjawi, who served in Jerusalem from 1923 to 1948. He asked Archbishop Samuel what it was he had found. Archbishop Samuel immediately realized what the Bedouin was holding and after some bartering, Archbishop Samuel bought the five scrolls, written in part Hebrew and part Aramaic. What the archbishop bought were the Dead Sea Scrolls. Among those scrolls was the famous Book of Isaiah, referred to as the Qumran Find.

Although their numbers are greatly reduced in Israel, I think the presence of Syrian Orthodox Christians in the Middle East is essential for their faith. I believe in their strength and their ability to survive under adverse circumstances as evidenced throughout their tumultuous history. They are productive members of society and practise their Christianity not only within the confines of the Church, but in their daily life as well. To me, they are an excellent example of Christian brotherhood.

Circassian, Israel—
Lynda Hoyle Still — ©
FRSA 1988

A CIRCASSIAN WOMAN

The historical background of the Circassians (also known as Cherkess) is the same Russian history described in the "Bukharan Dancer" chapter. The problems of political tyranny and religious persecution by the rulers were experienced by the cultures both of the Circassian Christians and Bukharan Jews.

The Caucasus range is one of the most rugged mountain barriers of the world. A natural bulwark separating Europe from Asia, it runs 750 miles, from the Sea of Azov to the Caspian Sea. It features several glaciers and the highest peak in Europe (18,481 feet), on Mount Elbrus.

Several ethnic groups live in the Caucasus area today. They primarily consist of Georgians, Nakh, Abkhaz-Adgey, Dagestan and the Turkic group which includes the Azerbaidjanis and Armenians.

Their mineral springs lead the list of natural resources. The most popular springs are situated in Pyatigorsk, Kislovodsk, and another in the Sochi area, dubbed the Russian Riviera. The Caucasus is rich in oil at either end (Baku and Maikop) as well as coal, manganese, lead, zinc and silver.

The Greeks are thought to be the first group to occupy this region. According to Greek legend, "Prometheus was chained to a Caucasus rock", and, "Jason and the Argonauts sought the Golden Fleece in Colchis". The Caucasus was subjected to invasion by the Romans, Persians (Iranians), Moslems and Mongols up to the 16th century, followed by the Turks and, again, the Iranians.

The Circassians, then Christians, lived in the northwest area of these mountains between Kuban and the Black Sea. Until the 15th century they were known as Kasogs, and were later called Circassians.

With so many invasions of this mountainous region, once the Cherkess Autonomous Oblast (a political subdivision of Caucassia in the former USSR), the linguistic complexities of the area are quite understandable.

Our group, the Circassians, shared an individual language group with their cousins the Karbadians. The language family group is Japhetic, which includes their particular dialect called Adyge. For subsistence they grew wheat, corn and sunflowers. They did lumbering as well, but the area is best known for its flour, dairy and food products in addition to cement, sodium sulphate, shoes, furniture and clothing.

Unfortunately, most of the history of the Circassians remains unwritten. I, therefore, will present you with the information received during my visits and interviews with Yaffa, a teacher of history and geography in the village of Kafr Kama, Israel.

The subject of the painting is Fatima, a resident of this village and a widow. She did not allow the sitting for her portrait to disturb her normal routine of caring for her grandchildren. While being sketched, she held a small child in her lap and, with her foot, rocked the cradle of another infant grandchild.

What Yaffa related about their history is consistent with what I have already written. The Circassians were tired and felt desolate as a result of all the invasions and occupations. During the Ottoman era, the Turks needed good soldiers and horsemen to protect their interests in the colonies. They promised the Circassians a better life and work if they left the Caucasus and migrated to Turkey. By this time, many of the Circassians had already converted to Islam (Sunni sect), and those Christians who left the Caucasus were converted to Islam in Turkey. They travelled through the Balkans to reach Turkey. Once the Circassians were there, the Turkish government sent many of them to Syria, Jordan, Lebanon, Egypt and a small number to Palestine, to be scouts, guards and soldiers for them. In Palestine, the Circassians settled into four villages, Hadera, Caesaria, Rechania (near Safed) and Kafr Kama.

Today, the Circassian population in the Holy Land is about 3,000. Two hundred live in Kafr Kama and the balance are spread among the other communities. Kafr Kama, however, is considered the center of the Circassians in the Holy Land.

These people have lived here for more than 100 years. There are also Circassian communities in Europe and the United States. I was told there are an estimated 8 million Circassians in Turkey, but this figure cannot be corroborated because census-taking in Turkey does not specify ethnicity. From my interviews with Yaffa, you will understand more about the Circassians living in Turkey further along in the chapter. Another million Circassians live in the Middle East and 2 to 3 million in the United States and Europe. If these figures are correct, with a total of 10 to 11 million Circassians throughout the world, they are anything but an endangered culture. In the United States, most of the Circassians are concentrated in Paterson, New Jersey. They don't have a mosque there, but have converted a house into a type of mosque, without adornment of the dome or the traditional four minarets. I have been informed that a new mosque and school have recently been constructed in New Jersey, replete with the traditional dome and four minarets. I made several attempts to visit these people but was denied access to the community.

While in Palestine, the Circassians worked primarily as farmers and, for the most part, continue the same work today. In or around 1986, a sweater factory was established in the community by a Brazilian woman named Edna Ross. She and her husband Shevach established the factory and all the intricate handwork is done only by the very talented and hard-working Circassian women.

During the Turkish occupation of Palestine, the Circassians were conscripted as soldiers. When the British took control, they fought with the British troops, and when these forces left in 1948, many Circassians joined the Israeli army.

There is very little contact between the Circassians in Israel and those in neighboring countries. This causes them a great deal of stress, since many families have been split.

The Kafr Kama community is orthodox Sunni Moslems. Like the Druze, they have a very closed society to protect their culture and history and they follow their tradition very seriously. They marry within their own ethnic group. There are some cases of Jewish girls converting to Islam, but very few conversions of Jewish males. It is even rare for a Circassian to intermarry with a member of another Sunni Moslem sect. They claim that, although both sects believe in Islam, their customs, habits and culture are totally different. In fact, their only similarity is their mutual belief in Islam. They have a matriarchal society and every request or desire seems to come through the women. For example, if Yusef wants a favor of someone, he will always say, "Sarah says ..."

During my most recent visit to Kafr Kama (March, 1990), I was bringing regards from some Circassians in the United States to two men of the village. I told one of the ladies that I wished to greet these men. She acknowledged that she knew them, took the greetings and I was not privileged to actually meet them myself.

The Circassians do not feel obligated to go to Mecca. When I asked Yaffa if the Circassians respect someone who has made the pilgrimage a little more, her reply was, "We respect the man or woman for what he or she is and not because they went to Mecca. There is a great respect for elders, but not because they may or may not have made the pilgrimage."

As an example of the difference in the practice of their religion and that of other Sunni Moslems, Yaffa mentioned that Circassian boys and girls openly plan parties together, with the parents in attendance, and dance traditional dances together. This is strictly forbidden by the Koran. It could be said that the Circassians are superficially following the tenets of Islam. I witnessed a wedding party in this same village and, although couples were dancing together, I observed that neither partner touched the other.

Yaffa went on to explain that many of their special customs (that is, festivities for each season of the year) are no longer held since the Circassians have become somewhat assimilated into the secular society. However, they still have their own language and a special dance peculiar to them. The dance is called Cherkosia. The solo male dancer places his hands on his hips, palms out, nods to a female (only unmarried females may participate) in the circle, as in a ring, creating a dance floor (which could be the main road of the village) and the male prances around the female in the style of dressage (fancy and intricate horse steps). The female, also with her hands on her hips, palms out, seems to float around, teasing him on. When the man is tired, he thanks his partner and returns to the ring while another male takes his place, continuing the ritual. There was one other dance I observed toward the end of the evening, performed only by males, and I was told that it was called the Debka. It reminded me of the Kazachok I have seen performed by many other Russian ethnic groups. In this dance, the males squat, hands on hips and, in tempo with the sprightly music, kick out one foot at a time while hopping on the bent leg. As adventurous as I would like to think I am, I had no inclination to try this feat.

When I asked Yaffa about her expectations for the future of the Circassians, her eyes misted over. The intent of my question was to learn if she felt they would continue to exist as a separate religious sect in Israel or eventually be absorbed by the secular Western culture surrounding them. Her answer took me by surprise. She said the Circassians seriously dream that one day they will be reunited and return to their own land, just as did the Jews after being absent for so long. Even as the Jews dreamed about the Holy Land, their dream is to return to the Caucasus Mountains. They are not suffering or hungry, but simply yearn for their own homeland. Even though generations of her family were born in Israel, they continue to regret that they were not born in their own land. She said that if the Soviets permit them to return, they will not return as Soviets. They want to be autonomous and not under any rule but Circassian.*

Her attitude toward her homeland is that even if it is not the best, it is still her own. She quoted Theodor Herzl (the founder of the Zionist movement) when he said, "If you want it, it's not a fantasy", meaning if you want something badly enough the fantasy will become a reality.

What was also interesting in my conversation with Yaffa was that, even though there may be 8 million Circassians in Turkey, those 8 million do not enjoy the freedom of the 3,000 living in Israel. In Israel they are permitted to be Circassians in every sense of the word – religion, dress, language and customs. In Turkey, they are considered Turks and are not allowed to speak their language outside their homes. They cannot behave like a large minority; they must be like all the other Turks. This is probably the answer to the question of why the Turkish census, as previously mentioned, does not specify ethnicity.

The village administration is conducted by elected members of the community. Elections are held every four years and the officers not only conduct the affairs of the village, but attend to any disputes arising within the community. These officials are recognized by the government of Israel as the official representatives of the village.

Marriage in this group is in the form of kidnaping. This is an ancient and traditional custom. Today it is more of a game, but in the past it was a true kidnap. The kidnap is carried out for either of two reasons. The first reason is in keeping with the tradition; the second is when someone in the family objects to the marriage. The young couple arranges to meet somewhere and the man takes the woman to the home of one of his relatives. It is then *fait accompli*. A messenger is sent to the parents of the bride, who appear to be angry and do not attend the wedding, which occurs a day after the kidnap and only after the bride and groom sign a marriage contract between themselves. The date of the contract is the wedding date. Until this contract is signed, the couple does not cohabit. Two weeks after the marriage, they return to the bride's parents' home to "make peace". They then go to the house of the groom's family and live there until they can build their own home or rent an apartment.

---

* It is now more than two-and-a-half years since my interview with Yaffa, and, while I write of the Circassian's dream, ethnic wars between the Azerbaidjanis and Armenians are still going on in the former USSR.

The more modern wedding ceremony I attended involved no kidnaping. When everything was agreed upon by the families of the bride and groom, a contract was drawn up. The signing of the contract is the same as taking vows and the couple is considered married. However, the bride stays in her parents' home for thirty days. When this period has elapsed, the groom leaves his house, accompanied by friends and family, to take the bride to his house. All the female relatives of the bride are waiting with her while the groom's procession parades through the streets, clapping hands and playing accordions. The bride will not see her mother for two weeks and the mother does not attend the wedding party. So when her daughter leaves, it is with sadness, at least outwardly. The procession returns to the groom's house with the bride. Well-wishers throw coins from their homes along the way. The bride (and the procession) stops to collect the coins. This was the ceremony I was privileged to attend. As you can see, their respect for tradition is in this form of marriage as well.

Upon arrival at the groom's house, the invited guests are ushered to an area where they are served a sumptuous meal while the bride is settled into a specially decorated room just for her. Outside on the street, friends, family and any villager who wishes, begin the dancing and music-making I described earlier. This goes on for hours. I remember asking when the dancers would break for some food. I was told that the entire village had been served a feast in the afternoon and this meal we were served was prepared for special guests. I did feel special and was grateful to be invited to participate in this colorful and happy occasion.

As I mentioned earlier, Yaffa teaches geography and history in the community of Kafr Kama. The Ministry of Education directs the schools in a basic curriculum in accordance with the entire school system of the country. Yaffa said if there is sufficient time, additional studies are introduced into the curriculum.

Israel
Gabra
Lunda
Hayle
Gill—©
FRSA 1999

96

A SABRA (RUTH DAYAN)

Our subject, Ruth Dayan, nee Schwarz, is the daughter of Russian-born intellectuals who emigrated from Russia as children in the early 1900s. Her mother was brought to Palestine by her parents when she was eight years of age. Her father was sent alone to Palestine by his parents when he was only fourteen because they were afraid he might become a Russian revolutionary; they preferred he become a Zionist.

Her maternal grandfather, Boris Klimker, was a Sorbonne-trained chemical engineer. He established an oil factory in Palestine and became one of Israel's first capitalists. Her maternal grandmother, Pnina, became a nurse and a midwife, working with Arab patients in Safed and Nablus, where, at the time, a Jewish professional woman must have seemed strangely out of place. Pnina and Boris were freethinkers and political liberals, and this thinking was passed on to Ruth's parents and, ultimately, to Ruth.

Ruth's parents met while attending Palestine's first Hebrew high school, the Herzliya Gymnasium in Tel Aviv. Although the school was to be known as a hotbed of free thought, it also proved to be the spawning ground of many of Israel's future leaders. With such soon-to-be-famous social activists as Moshe Sharett, Dov Has, Eliahu Golomb and Itzhak Olshan, they organized a secret society, swearing to devote their lives to the country's service. Under the very noses of the oppressive Turkish regime which then ruled Palestine, the seeds of the Haganah (the future defense force of the Jewish community in Palestine) were sown by Dov Has, who later would be instrumental in the formation of Israel's air force.

Social justice, equal rights for women, a "natural and anti-materialistic" way of life and love based on freedom rather than conventional rules were some of the principles espoused by these precocious teenagers. But despite the practice of "free love" by their peers, Ruth's mother and father opted to marry soon after graduation.

Ruth was born in Haifa on March 6, 1917, less than a year before the Balfour Declaration – the results of which would inexorably shape the rest of Ruth's life as a pioneer, a wife of the renowned Moshe Dayan, a mother of three and an ardent participant in her country's struggle for freedom and peace.

Now, not to digress, but rather to present the panoply of events which would make Ruth a product of her times and society, I think it germane to discuss the history of Zionism and the key players in the convoluted geopolitical game which led to the now-infamous Balfour Declaration.

Before the Russian pogroms of 1881, the fragmented Jewish communities throughout the Diaspora looked optimistically forward toward eventual assimilation into their host countries. But after these atrocities, only those Jews who lived in England or emigrated to America (in vast numbers) could realistically aspire to integration. Yet, even in America, the sudden influx of some 2 million refugee Jews, most of whom were Yiddish-speaking (a combination of several languages, basically German), Orthodox or Hassidic, impoverished and terrified, created a feeling of fear and apprehension among the American-minded, largely Reformist American Jewry. They anticipated, correctly, that the overwhelmingly Protestant Christian population would transfer their anti-Catholic prejudices to a wave of anti-Semitism. Paradoxically, despite the spread of such anti-Semitic subcultures as the Ku Klux Klan, the flood of disadvantaged Ashkenazi (Eastern European) Jews who settled in the lower east side of New York City soon established themselves as a proud, vibrant community. Like Phoenix rising from the ashes, they built a power base in this refuge from which the cause of worldwide Jewry would soon develop a new and resonant chorus of voices.

The "lead singer" among the American Jews was Emma Lazarus (1849-87), whose timeless sonnet graces the Statue of Liberty:

> Give me your tired, your poor,
> Your huddled masses yearning to breathe free,
> The wretched refuse of your teeming shore.
> Send these, the homeless, tempest-toss't to me.
> I lift the lamp beside the golden door.

Paul Johnson, in his *A History Of The Jews*, writes: "It was as though history was slowly solving a great jigsaw puzzle, slipping the pieces into their place one after another. The American mass Jewry was one piece. The next piece was the Zionist idea."

The concept of an idealized Jewish community is as old as the Babylonian exile. The original Zionists were religious zealots. The new Zionism, which was triggered by the Russian atrocities of 1881, was more a movement of secularists than Messianics. But Zionism in all its forms had one common goal: the establishment of a nation-state in or around Jerusalem.

This would call for colonization, however, a process without which a new Zion could never hope to emerge. Since, at the time, Great Britain was not only sympathetic to the Zionist concept, but had already voiced its support in the writings of her Foreign Secretary, Lord Palmerston, and two novels by her Sephardic (those people coming from the Mediterranean basin) Prime Minister, Benjamin Disraeli, the Zionists sought their sponsorship. Fortunately, George Eliot had recently published her novel, (yes, her name was George) *Daniel Deronda*, which so persuasively urged bringing the Diaspora back to Palestine to form a new nation. Her timing could not have been more fortuitous for the Zionist cause. The novel was internationally acclaimed, widely read and so moved Arthur Balfour, the Conservative leader of Parliament, that he became a staunch supporter of Zionism. With such influential British parliamentarians as Winston Churchill and David Lloyd George ascribing to the establishment of a Jewish nation-state, the one element lacking was a charismatic Jewish leader – a living embodiment of Eliot's hero, Daniel Deronda.

It was a Viennese journalist named Theodor Herzl (1860-1904) who was to become the driving force of modern Zionism. In January, 1895, while covering the court martial and public humiliation of Captain Alfred Dreyfus in Paris, Herzl's life was forever changed. He watched in disbelief as Dreyfus, the only Jewish officer on the French army's general staff, who had been indicted on fabricated evidence, was convicted of giving military secrets to the Germans. As he was being marched about the courtyard of the Ecole Militaire, Dreyfus loudly proclaimed his innocence. The immense crowd which had gathered outside heard his protestations, and as Herzl left the building he was shocked to hear the mob chanting, "Death to Dreyfus! Death to the Jews!"

Hitherto an assimilationist who had considered such extreme avenues to acceptance as a pact with the Pope which would "trade" conversion of masses of Jews to Catholicism in exchange for a papal campaign against anti-Semitism, Herzl was so dismayed by the Dreyfus incident that he wrote a book (*Der Judenstaat*) in which he disavowed his assimilative posture and proposed the establishment of a sovereign Jewish state.

So charismatic and theatrical that some of the most powerful rabbis in Europe called him "the one called by God". Herzl quickly attracted a following of *Ostjuden* (the poor huddled masses of Ashkenazi refugees), who had been forced to abandon hope of ever being citizens of Russia or Poland. The young David Ben-Gurion considered Herzl the Messiah. To Chaim Weizman, then a college student in Berlin, Herzl's message was like "a bolt from the blue". An army of eastern Jews rallied around Herzl and gathered together in Basel for the First Zionist Congress in 1897. Although the Congress was snubbed by the middle-class, Western Jewish contingent, Herzl attracted special correspondents from twenty-six newspapers. Among the new constituency which embraced this charismatic zealot, the professional politicians and organizers who became Herzl's lieutenants, there was an awareness of his ingenuousness. These men, who eventually would take over the movement, privately snickered at the foppish Herzl's "frock-coat Zionism", but they were pragmatic enough to encourage him in his role of Messiah. He was an accomplished diplomat at the personal level, the epitome of respectability, and blessed with a presence that could be taken seriously. When it was made evident to Herzl that Turkey and Germany were anti-Zionist, Herzl turned to the generally pro-Jewish British elite, impressing the political establishment with a paper he wrote for the British Cabinet exhorting them to establish a homeland for the dispossessed Jews. As a result, he won a major concession: diplomatic recognition for a prototypical Zionist state.

After Herzl's untimely death in 1904, Dr Chaim Weizman became the most effective spokesman for Zionism in the West. Emigrating to England around the turn of the century, where he became a highly respected teacher of biochemistry, Weizman became a British citizen in 1910. He cultivated friendships with publishers and members of Parliament at a most propitious time: just before the outbreak of World War I. Not only did key British politicians favor the Zionist cause for humanitarian reasons, but also for the pragmatic purpose of preventing Germany or France from establishing a foothold in the oil-rich Middle East.

In January, 1917, British troops launched the invasion of Palestine. Also, as fate would have it, the Russian Czar was overthrown in the very same month and year, and Russia's provisional Prime Minister Kerensky disavowed Russia's anti-Semitic code. These two events garnered worldwide Jewish support for the Allied cause, and, shortly thereafter, the Balfour Declaration was drafted.

In its original form, the declaration contained three major provisions: the recognition of Palestine (in its entirety) as the national home of the Jews; internal autonomy for the Jews in Palestine; and the unrestricted right of Jewish immigration.

However, because of the vociferous objections raised by the influential Edwin Montagu, a banker, politician and vehement anti-Zionist Jew, the final draft was revised drastically by the British War Cabinet. It now made no mention of a national home for Jews, it made no reference to unlimited immigration or Jewish internal autonomy and it insisted upon safeguarding the rights of the Palestinian Arabs.

Flawed as it was, the Balfour Declaration was the cornerstone upon which the Jewish state would be built.

Ironically, it was published the same year that Ruth Schwarz, our subject, was born. The shortcomings for the Jews of this well-intentioned but fatally compromised document would determine the destiny of this sabra child – and indeed of all Israeli Jews – for generations.

In 1918, after the British had defeated the Turkish forces in northern Palestine, Ruth's parents were ordered by the secret society to go to London to study. Anticipating that the new Jewish nation would need leaders with higher education, they studied English in addition to their respective majors: her father concentrated on political science and rabbinical studies; her mother majored in chemistry. As a consequence of the family's eight-year residency in London, Ruth and her sister Reumah were fluent in Hebrew and English, and, thanks to both their parents' knowledge of Arabic, they were conversant in that language as well. These linguistic abilities would serve both girls well in the future.

When the Schwarz family returned to Palestine in October, 1926, Ruth found it difficult to adjust to the homeland of which she had no recollection. The village of Musrara, which is the first home Ruth remembers, was close to the Old City of Jerusalem. Thrust into this predominantly Arabic community, Ruth was traumatized by the noise, the rudeness and the lack of respect Palestinian schoolchildren displayed in the classroom. She felt more of a stranger in her homeland than she had in London. Consequently, she stayed away from school as often as possible.

Eventually she joined the Girl Scouts, which helped her overcome her feelings of loneliness and apartness. Her parents, delighted to be back in Palestine, busied themselves with their respective careers: he as a lecturer, she as the organizer of an after-school playground for both Arab and Jewish children.

In the summer of 1930, Ruth met a brilliant teenager named Zvi Toledano, who, like most of his young peers, was already an ardent, revolver-carrying member of the Haganah (the foundation of the Israeli Defense Forces, or IDF).

The first love in Ruth's life, this sensitive, poetic, yet heroic youth was destined to become a Haganah hero and martyr in 1941. At the age of 26, as a member of "the 23" aboard the *Sea Lion*, he participated in a British raid on Tripoli, Lebanon. The ship and crew vanished without a trace. But the heroic Zvi and his crewmates will forever hold a place of reverence in Israeli military history.

The platonic romance with Zvi ended after two years. Ruth remembers that her socialist idealism and her totally kibbutznik (collective farm) philosophy was an irreconcilable difference that even their intense love for one another could not overcome.

Convinced that she should take an active role in the kibbutz movement, Ruth dropped out of high school and enrolled in the Nahalal Agricultural School for Girls, near Haifa. Here she met a young farmer named Moshe Dayan, whose ideology and personality were quite different from Ruth's. Moshe and his parents lived on a moshav, a quite different form of farming and industrial collective. (All the members of a moshav own their land, own their individual homes and earn their money according to their individual productivity; in a kibbutz, however, the accent is on team effort for the collective good with little emphasis on personal ownership of goods and property.)

Ruth's romantic approach to farming was something she never lost, despite the backbreaking chores and the blistered hands. And after marrying Moshe Dayan on July 12, 1935, she happily anticipated a quiet life as a farmer's wife – the sort of idyllic partnership she had dreamed of since childhood. What she would not let herself think about were the growing tensions between the Arabs, the Jews and the British which would soon erupt into violent confrontations and, eventually, war.

Despite stringent immigration quotas imposed on the Jews by the British, the Jewish settlement in Palestine grew rapidly in the 1930s. This so incensed the Arabs that they started a campaign of terrorism against the Jews and British in Palestine. This bloody action became known as the Riots of 1936-39. They began in Jaffa in April, 1936, and spread like wildfire throughout the country. Hundreds of people were killed or wounded and thousands of acres of farmland were destroyed. In an attempt to paralyze the economy, the Arab High Committee declared a general strike. But after 175 days during which no Arab reported for work and all Arab-owned businesses remained closed, the Jews were able to report that they had actually stepped up production to such an extent that the Arab strike constituted no threat to the economy.

In 1936, the Dayans moved to a new moshav called Shimron. Situated on a hill above Nahalal, it was comparatively safe from the marauding Arabs and, for a time, Moshe could devote his time and energies to farming alongside Ruth. But when the Arabs began attacking the British, the latter expanded the Jewish police force and Moshe was enrolled as a sergeant. He began spending most of his time in training and, except for the first few idyllic months in Shimron, Ruth saw little of her husband. Moshe's qualities as a military leader were soon recognized by the British and, as a result, he was accepted for further Haganah training. Ruth could not know it at the time, but she had married the man who would go down in history as the greatest military leader in Israeli history.

Ironically, when the British trained the Haganah to help them put down the Arab riots, they were training the very men who would one day turn against them.

Although Jewish brigades fought valiantly at the side of the Allied forces in World War II, the seeds of Jewish discontent had been sown when the British issued new regulations against immigration in 1939. During the war, the British refused to allow the immigration of Jews from Nazi-controlled countries, fearing the infiltration of spies. This made it extremely difficult to rescue those Jews who managed to escape from the Nazis. Many ships sank trying to bring refugees to Palestine or after being turned away by the British. One of these ships, *Struma*, went down in the Black Sea in February, 1942, carrying 800 Jewish refugees to their deaths.

After World War II, the new Labour government in England, and especially Foreign Minister Ernest Bevin, opted not to ease the restrictions on Jewish immigration. But what strained Anglo-Jewish relations to the breaking point was the British decision to move regiments of British soldiers to Palestine to prevent the survivors of the Holocaust from entering the country. Only now did the entire Jewish community realize that, "the war is over, but our war continues".

There were several Jewish paramilitary organizations in Palestine at this time: the Haganah (the major security force); the Palmach, a branch of the Haganah; the Etzel, an underground organization dedicated to the constant resistance to the British; and Lehi, a splinter organization of Etzel. These groups conjoined to form the Hebrew Movement of the Revolt. Their first assault upon the British took place on October 10, 1945, when illegal immigrants were released by force from a detention camp. There followed many sorties against radar stations, airfields and coastguard ships.

In 1939, Moshe and forty-two other young Haganah members were apprehended by the British police, accused of the illegal possession of weapons, tried and sentenced to ten years in prison. But two years later, when the British army needed all the soldiers it could get, "the 43" as they were known, were abruptly released. While some of the pardoned prisoners joined the British army, Moshe was conscripted for a dangerous secret assignment by the Haganah. In an action near the Lebanese border, his binoculars were struck by a bullet, embedding metal into the eye socket and resulting in the loss of that eye. Because reconstructive surgery, even if successful, would serve only a cosmetic purpose, Moshe accepted the disfigurement. The black eye-patch he wore thereafter became a symbol of courage to the IDF (Israeli Defense Force) he led through the three wars which followed the Arabs' rejection of the United Nations' partitioning of Palestine in 1947.

Since this book has no pretensions of being a history of Israel, suffice it to say that Moshe Dayan's inspiring leadership through the War of Independence (1948), the Six-Day War (1967) and the Yom Kippur War (1973) stamped him as one of the greatest military tacticians in history.

Perhaps it was inevitable that Moshe's preoccupation with his career would create an ever-widening breach between this living legend and his family.

Ruth's social consciousness, combined with her celebrity as the wife of Moshe Dayan, propelled her into a series of cultural projects which attempted to bridge the gap of mistrust between Israelis and Arabs. Her thoughts on the Arab-Israeli problem, as she writes in her eloquent autobiography, *And Perhaps,* are worth quoting here:

"Some people in Israel believe that life would be simpler if there were no Arabs here. But the fact is they are here, and many families trace their roots back hundreds of years. What our wars – our victories and the Arab defeats –prove is that both sides must learn to live in peace. And this will happen only when the Arabs, even those who believe that endless wars bring nothing but endless suffering, learn to reread history."

When Ruth's marriage to General Dayan ended in divorce in 1971, this resilient and resourceful woman began a new and even more interesting period of her life. Maskit, an organization which provided facilities and instructions in arts and crafts to members of all ethnic groups, which Ruth cofounded (under the auspices of the Israeli government) in the 1960s, became a thriving network of cottage industries, providing supplemental income to thousands of weavers, embroiderers, jewelers, ceramicists, and so on. As the driving force behind Maskit, Ruth used her considerable influence throughout the world to promote and merchandise the many artistic and utilitarian items Maskit-trained artisans produced.

In 1978, Ruth was appointed Handicraft Consultant to the Inter-American Development Bank in Washington, DC, where, for five years, she planned projects similar to Maskit for Guatemala, Ecuador, Peru, Haiti, Paraguay Uruguay, the Dominican Republic, El Salvador, Brazil and Argentina, generating thousands of jobs for the disadvantaged. With the volunteer assistance of dedicated professional experts (most of them from Israel) in such crafts as ceramics, weaving, fashion design and so on, new and better techniques were introduced, all of which were aimed at making small arts-and-crafts businesses more viable.

Returning to Israel in 1983, Ruth created and developed, among other projects, an organization of twelve Israeli professionals which established mobile training shops in Bophuthatswana, which reached out to remote villages to train instructors, who, in turn, after two years of instruction, continued the mobile shop concept, teaching hundreds of students to become skilled artists and artisans.

Today, Ruth Dayan is a legend in her own right. Now in her seventies, this indefatigable humanitarian is incredibly active in many charities and business organizations. She is president of the Israeli Designer/Craftsmen Association, representing Israel in The World Craft Council. She is president of Brith B'nei Shem, which fosters the peaceful coexistence of Arabs and Jews in Israel. She is president of the Friends of the Academy for Art Teachers in Ramat Hasharon and a member of the Board of Governors of the Bezalel Academy of Arts and Design. As if all of the above is not enough, Ruth has taken a new immigrant under her wings and together they opened the Tamaru House of Crafts. From a rented house they forged a gallery that is breathtaking to the eyes of anyone visiting. This handicraft gallery serves as an outlet for artisans worldwide and, of course, in Israel. They have captured the hearts of the globe with visitors from every conceivable country, and have been written about in several magazines and newspapers in Israel and in several international publications.

Ruth Dayan has lived – and is continuing to live – an adventurous and fulfilling life.

If I have gained nothing else from writing this book, I shall forever feel amply rewarded for having known Ruth, fallen in love with her and been privileged to write this chapter about her. She is truly a remarkable woman.

Susan holding a baby Bedouin boy, a typical two-year-old.

DIARY

FEBRUARY 15, 1988: I arrived in Israel with my husband Elisha to begin working on the book. I preceded Lunda by three months, hoping to make all the arrangements for my interviews and her paintings before her arrival. But the only thing I was able to organize was her bedroom. One would imagine that making contact with ten people from ten different cultures would be a simple matter. It was not. Despite three months of researching, writing letters and telephoning, I was able to obtain but one firm commitment, an appointment with Bracha Eliezerov, the Bukharan dancer, thanks to the help of Nitza Bahrouzi, a curator at the Museum of Israel in Tel Aviv.

It was not until I called my friend Essia Steinfeld and vented my frustrations and anguish on her that anyone suggested I contact Ruth Dayan. Perhaps, like me, most of my acquaintances considered this great woman to be an icon, unapproachable. My initial reaction to Essia's suggestion was to laugh and exclaim, "Are you crazy? Me call Ruth Dayan? That's like saying, 'Call Nancy Reagan!'" Essia tried to explain that things were different in Israel, that there was no protocol to be observed in contacting Mrs Dayan, and that with her years of experience in dealing with many cultures, she could and would be of inestimable help to my project. But I was so intimidated by the name Dayan that I could not summon the nerve to act on Essia's suggestion.

A few days later, Elisha and I were invited to a dinner at Essia's house, where I was seated opposite a charming lady, Shula Prihar, the wife of a retired Israeli general. When she learned of the problems I had encountered in my project, she asked me, "Why don't you call Ruth Dayan?" I replied that, since I did not know Mrs Dayan personally, I could not bring myself to just pick up the phone and call her. Nothing more was said of the matter, but as luck would have it, Essia asked Elisha if we would mind driving the general and his wife home. We were happy to oblige, and the Prihars thanked us profusely for the favor. "No big deal," Elisha insisted as we bade them good night. The next morning, over my first cup of coffee, I was agonizing about calling this famous personage, Ruth Dayan. Normally, I have no trouble calling total strangers on matters of importance, but even though I had been given her phone number, I just could not summon the chutzpah to dial it. Then the phone jangled next to me, snapping me out of my reverie. It was Shula Prihar calling to thank us for the ride last night and to tell me that Ruth Dayan was waiting for my call! That same day, Ruth Dayan and I sat across my dining-room table. Over lunch we discussed my project and my need for access to the various cultural groups I wanted to include in my book. Not only did Ruth agree to help me, she personally arranged meetings for us with the Druze sheik and the Circassian woman subjects we used. Ruth became so interested in our work that she accompanied Lunda and me on several of our field trips.

APRIL 18: Thanks to the suggestion of an author friend, Dalia Weinstein Blumenfeld, I was introduced to Dantchu Arnon, an accomplished photographic journalist, who very quickly became our friend and my invaluable assistant. Dantchu's work had gained him access to many cultures in Israel, and it was he who arranged our meetings with the desert Bedouin, the Hassidic rabbi, the Samaritans, the Circassian wedding couple and the Ethiopian girl in Safed. The Syrian Orthodox Christian subject was contacted by me, and the sabra (Ruth Dayan) somewhat reluctantly allowed us to use her as a subject.

APRIL 19-27: Lunda arrived on the 19th. After a few days of showing her about Tel Aviv, visiting the port of Jaffa and introducing her to Ruth, Dantchu and a few of our friends, we took her to meet two of our kibbutznik acquaintances, Nathan and Yael, who live on Kibbutz Maabarot (Maabarot means passages or transition – a place for refugees). We were fascinated by Yael's 82-year-old mother, Gusti Melzer, who in 1933 had been one of the first kibbutzniks. Her stories of building the kibbutz despite Arab raids, traveling through hostile territory to Jerusalem to learn Hebrew and learning to farm without the proper tools or knowledge made us realize how much sweat and blood had been spilled to build this harsh land into the thriving industrial and agricultural nation it is today.

APRIL 27: Our first appointment. It was with the Bukharan dancer, Bracha Eliezerov. Our subject was recalcitrant at first, but once we got her to play her music, she was transformed into an animated, vibrant subject. Lunda was quite pleased with her painting and I was deeply touched by her personal story. We knew now that my book and the paintings had a meaningful purpose.

APRIL 29: Our trip to Mount Gerizim turned out to be quite an adventure. After I spent most of the preceding day preparing sandwiches and drinks (and Lunda prepared her canvases and paints), Elisha, our "Commanding Officer", awakened us at 6.15 a.m. to make sure that we were ready to leave at 7.00. We left at 7.30, much to my ex-soldier husband's consternation.

Dantchu and his wife Nomi had previously arranged with Elisha to meet us "somewhere along the way". This sort of non-specific planning was to be repeated on several subsequent trips, and it never ceased to amaze Lunda and me that Elisha always managed to be at the right spot at the right time. In some of the desolate areas we traversed, it's astonishing we ever met at all!

Lunda paints the portrait of a Samaritan, while I record the anthropological and historical information.

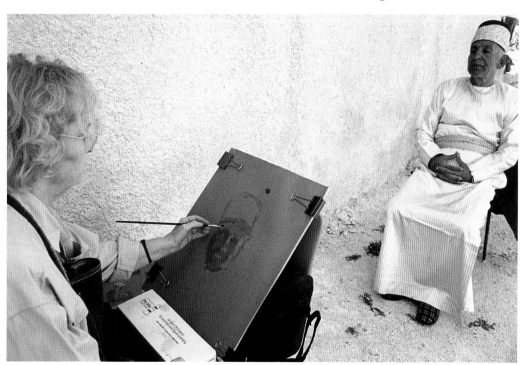

By the time we arrived at Mount Gerizim, we were famished. We looked about for a place to sit and enjoy our picnic lunch. Then we were told that all the Samaritans were fasting. What we had failed to realize was that, because this was a leap year, the Jewish Passover had taken place a month earlier than the Samaritans', as the Samaritans follow a different calendar. Because of the imminent holiday, the Samaritans abstained from eating leavened bread – the very stuff of which our delicious sandwiches were made. We tried "sneak eating" behind parked cars, but there seemed always to be a fasting Samaritan watching us. How embarrassing! We finally packed it all in and took one of the cars farther up the mountain. There, at last, we enjoyed an undisturbed lunch and got an amazing view of Nablus (Shechem) below us. Then, from the very top of the mountain, we were able to see some of the Samaritans' holy places, which Dantchu pointed out to us. These sites included the spot where, supposedly, Abraham had prepared to sacrifice his only son to show his loyalty to God. Very impressive.

We returned to the Samaritan village in time to witness the paschal lamb ceremony, which I describe in the "Samaritan" chapter. Then, by one of our many strokes of good fortune, we stumbled upon the High Priest, who became the subject of Lunda's painting and my interview.

After a long and exciting day, we returned to Tel Aviv for a well-earned night's rest.

MAY 1: Lunda had been scheduled to paint an urban Bedouin. But when we called to reconfirm, her husband said she was not well, so we cancelled. Instead, Lunda painted our Nigerian houseman, Ezekiel. She gave him the painting, and, from his reaction to the gift, I imagine it is now his most prized possession. He calls the painting his "silent brother".

That evening, Yossi and Julie Harel gave a dinner party for Lunda. In 1947, Yossi had been the Chief of Security aboard the ship *Exodus*, whose ill-fated attempt to smuggle 4,500 illegal immigrants from France into Palestine resulted in tragedy (the British, then in control of Palestine, returned the passengers to Hamburg, where many died in the camps for displaced people).

Other guests included Ezer and Reuma Weizman (he is now the President of Israel, was then the Minister of Science and Technology, and is the nephew of Chaim Weizman; Reuma is Ruth Dayan's younger sister), General and Mrs Gaby Prihar and several members of Parliament.

Although the party was given in Lunda's honor, most of the conversation was in Hebrew. As hard as I tried to get them to speak English, they automatically reverted back to Hebrew. Poor Lunda. She could not understand one word. But when I apologized for the guests' lack of consideration, she assured me she was having a wonderful time and thought our friends were lovely people. Lunda's main world is visual. She did enjoy studying their faces, and I guess the mere fact that all these dignitaries had come to honor her was enough. I explained to Lunda that my friends did not mean to be rude; but when you get a group of politicos together, it is bound to change the quietest tea party into an animated political harangue.

MAY 2-3:   Monday, May 2, we received a call from Dantchu. He had found a Hassidic Jew who was willing to come to Dantchu's studio and sit for Lunda. We were asked to wait for an exact time, but after standing by all day, we learned that the appointment was to be at 4.00 p.m. on Tuesday.

Since I knew how diffident Hassidim were about posing for photographers, I was beginning to wonder if the man was having second thoughts about posing for Lunda. So, it was with some trepidation that we arrived early Tuesday afternoon at Dantchu's studio in old Jaffa. We chatted with Dantchu and his partner, Tzvika, planning what other subject we might try to contact if my fears were realized and the Hassid didn't show up. Fortunately, our subject arrived promptly at four. Phew! What a relief! And what a perfect subject he turned out to be. Interestingly, although he posed willingly for Lunda's painting, he asked me not to videotape him. He had no objection to having still photographs shot of him, however, so long as they were candid shots – not posed portraits.

As it turned out, Lunda's likeness of him was so accurate, there was no mistaking his identity. I only hope the published book does not cause him any embarrassment in the Hassidic community.

MAY 4:   We arose early for our trip to Safed, which was to be a jam-packed two-day adventure, as it turned out. Dantchu had made arrangements for us to meet our Ethiopian subject in the morning, see the pre-Lag B'Omer celebrations in the afternoon, then drive up Mount Meron to witness the actual Lag B'Omer festivities that night. Since this was to be a two-day event, we had made reservations at a Safed hotel for the nights of the 4th and 5th. Ruth Dayan joined us for the ride to Safed, but would then leave us to visit friends in Tephen. She would rejoin us on the afternoon of the 5th to introduce us to the Circassian woman and the Druze sheik, whom she had contacted on our behalf and who would be the two subjects we would visit on the 6th.

We arrived in Safed at 8.30 a.m. Our first stop was at the home of Samuel and Miriam Perel, whose son was the mayor of Safed. Over coffee, the ebullient Miriam expounded on the virtues of Safed. She is a one-woman chamber of commerce and insisted we accompany her on a walking trip through town, ending at the cultural craft center which she helped establish for the Ethiopian immigrant community being settled in that area. By early afternoon, our Ethiopian subject had arrived. By any standards, she was exceptionally beautiful, even if initially shy, glum and uncooperative. I all but did somersaults to keep this woman sitting. Lunda and I were sure she would run out the door at any moment. Pressure was mounting, as we had to work fast to adhere to the tight schedule imposed on us by Dantchu's and Ruth's scheduling.

The pre-Lag B'Omer festivities wended through the streets of Safed all afternoon, with celebrants bearing Torah-carrying men on their shoulders to the accompaniment of singing, shouting, hand-clapping participants.

To explain the celebration of Lag B'Omer: from the second day of Passover (which celebrates the Jews' exodus from the Pharaohs of Egypt, and the beginning of the grain harvesting) until the end of Shavuot (the end of the cereal grain festival), there are forty-nine days. During these forty-nine days it was customary, in ancient times, to bring small amounts of grain to the temple as offerings. Also during these forty-nine days (referred to as the Sefira Days, because you count each day), it is forbidden to have any parties, weddings, haircuts, and so on. One explanation given is that a plague struck the students of Rabbi Akiva and only ceased on the thirty-third day of the Omer. This plague occurred during the rebellion against the Romans in 135 CE. This rebellion is known as the Bar Kochba Rebellion, named after the man who led the Jewish people. It is thought that many of Rabbi Akiba's students may have participated in this rebellion, and it is unclear whether there was actually a plague or the word was used to describe the destruction of these students. Many sources refer to this holiday as the Scholar's Day. It was during this same period that a man named Shimon Bar Yochai and his son hid in a cave on Mount Meron for twelve years to escape the Roman destruction. By some miracle they found a carob tree and survived by eating its fruit. It is thought that Shimon Bar Yochai died on the thirty-third day of the Omer in that cave. Rabbi Shimon Bar Yochai has been credited for writing the Zohar – a book on Jewish mysticism. The book was written during those twelve years.

From the Zohar came the Kabbalah. It is the Kabbalists (believers in Jewish mysticism) who hold to the belief in Rabbi Shimon Bar Yochai. His students, it is said, would dress as hunters to come visit him in the cave. At night they would light bonfires and celebrate. Whether you accept one or both versions it makes no difference because only on the thirty-third day of Lag B'Omer are celebrations allowed to be performed.

Now, how do we get to the thirty-third day, you ask? LAG has the numerical value of thirty-three. The first letter of the word is a *lamed,* which

Child peering out of apartment window at the festivities for Lag B'Omer taking place on the street below.

has a numerical value of thirty. The G, or *gimel*, is the third letter of the Hebrew alphabet and has a numerical value of three. The holiday is celebrated (especially on Mount Meron) by lighting bonfires in the evening, singing and praying. At daybreak they ceremoniously cut the hair of all little boys who have attained the age of three years. You may ask, "Why three?" and the only answer I can give would be some examples of the significance of the numbers three and seven in the Jewish religion. When a religious man prays he wears tefillin (phylacteries). They consist of two small boxes with leather straps holding them together. One box will be placed between the eyes and the other on the non-dominant hand. The straps keep them in place. The strap from the forehead hangs loose after going around the head. The other strap connecting the hand box is wound around the arm seven times (Creation and/or the biblical reference to the number seven can be found in Psalms 145:16), where seven Hebrew words make up that particular verse. The balance of the strap is wrapped around the hand three times, and then around the marriage finger three times. The Biblical reference to this can be found in Hosea 2:21-22. If you are really interested in those little black cubes, the Biblical references are Exodus 13:9 and 13:16, and Deuteronomy 6:8 and 11:18. Also, on the mezuzah there are three Hebrew letters – the *shin, daled* and *yud* (which is a synonym for God) – hung on the entrances to Jewish homes (and rooms within the home) to remind us of our loyalty and commitment to God. On Saturday afternoons, Mondays and Thursdays (the only midweek days the Torah is taken out of the holy ark to be read), Hanukkah, Purim and Fast days, three men only are called to read from the Torah. These blessings are called *aliyot* (to go up – the plural form). On all other occasions and holidays there can be seven *aliyot* given to the members of the congregation. These are but a few examples. Others have claimed that by the age of three the physical body is complete; that Moses was weaned at the age of three, and so on. I am assuming that all or any of the above allusions have some bearing on why the first haircut for Hassidic or Orthodox boys at three years of age.

On Wednesday night, May 4, we drove our two-car caravan to the foot of Mount Meron. Since Dantchu's little car had a "Press" sticker (and ours did not), we had to park the roomier BMW in a vast parking lot – among what seemed to be a million other cars. Then, like so many circus clowns, we squeezed into Dantchu's compact vehicle for the ride to the top of the mountain. You'd have thought we were going to the Super Bowl or the last game of the World Cup from the hundreds of buses, vans and automobiles in the "official" parking lot! Before parking his car, Dantchu let us off near the sea of bodies who were swarming about. Because of the milling throng, we arranged a time and place to meet. The meeting place was to be close to where Dantchu would be parking his car. The time was to be midnight.

Lunda, Elisha and I took a few deep breaths, then literally shouldered our way through the crowd and up the path toward the shrine. Kiosks and tents had been erected along both sides of the path. Everything imaginable, from food items to clothing and religious articles, was being loudly offered for sale. It was a Mardi Gras atmosphere, with hawkers using loudspeaker systems and bullhorns to proclaim the virtues of their products, while rabbis solicited donations for the support of their schools (*yeshivas*). We noticed that every tent and kiosk had some sort of sleeping arrangement, suggesting that this was to be a non-stop two-day event, and, already, some of the hardier participants had actually fallen asleep on concrete slabs!

When we finally muscled our way to the top of the mountain and entered the shrine, it was as if we had suddenly entered the world of mysticism. All sorts of praying and kabbalistic ritualism was going on. A series of contained fires was burning, with hundreds of people tossing lighted candles into them. The noise was so deafening I had to shout in Elisha's ear, "Let's get out of here!" He was happy to oblige, and we pushed our way outside to the comparative tranquility of the hawkers and rabbis.

We walked about, observing and taking photos, and realized strangely, the sustained excitement of the Hassidic celebrants was contagious.

Shortly before midnight, we all regrouped at the appointed place. We were utterly exhausted and ravenously hungry. We had been so caught up with the excitement, we forgot to eat. We then decided to wait until we returned to the hotel before eating. Our only problem now was to find Dantchu's car. It was not where he had parked it. After walking for what seemed like miles looking for it, Dantchu learned it had been towed to another field – and no one knew which one! Elisha and Dantchu decided that Dantchu would stay and continue searching for his car, while Elisha would take the women down the hill by taxi. By the time we reached the bottom, found our car and drove to the hotel, Dantchu had managed to find his car and return to the hotel long before we arrived. As we should have expected, the hotel kitchen was closed, as was every other eating place in Safed. Oh well, there was always breakfast to look forward to. We grumbled as we left the lighted lobby for the courtyard where our rooms were located – or so we thought. But the courtyard lights had been turned off, and there was no apparent numerical order to the rooms. Armed only with our room keys and a couple of mini-flashlights, we stumbled and groped about, searching for our rooms. Finally, we found three rooms which were unoccupied and which our keys would open. We appropriated the rooms, but, tired as I was, I slept fitfully through the night, half-expecting to be evicted by some irate concierge.

MAY 5:   After a huge breakfast at the hotel, we followed the same routine we established yesterday and returned to Mount Meron. Only, this time, Dantchu made certain that he parked his car in a proper parking area.

We were relieved to see that the mountain was less crowded and the atmosphere less frenetic that it had been the night before. We climbed to the shrine to watch the ceremonial haircutting ceremony. Fires were still burning and the hawkers were still hawking as the three-year-old boys were led to an enclosed area where the rabbis would make the first-ever cut of the youngster's hair. After watching a few clumsy snips, I remember thinking how fortunate the boys were that they were only getting their hair cut, not a circumcision. There were several professional barbers on hand, and they did their best to repair the damage the rabbis inflicted, thank goodness.

We left Mount Meron around two o'clock in the afternoon because Elisha had to collect Ruth Dayan at Tephen by 4.00 p.m.

On his way out of Safed, however, Elisha's car blew a tire. It took him more than an hour to locate a replacement tire, and for what it cost him, he figured he could have made a down payment on a good used car. But Elisha handles such inconveniences with great equanimity.

When he finally returned with Ruth, he bellowed a bit about paying a king's ransom for one stupid tire. He calmed down after a while and after some pleasant conversation with Ruth over tea, we spent the rest of the day sightseeing, having dinner at a pleasant little restaurant and planning our itinerary for the following day. Dantchu and his entourage had already begun their return to Tel Aviv.

MAY 6:   We left Safed a bit later than we had expected and arrived at the Circassian village of Kafr Kama at about 10.30 a.m. Here is where Lunda painted the Circassian woman Ruth had arranged for. Our group was now small, consisting of Ruth, Lunda, Elisha and me. Since the Circassians are Moslems and this was Friday (their Sabbath), we had to finish the Circassian interview and painting by 2.00 p.m. We met the deadline and, by mid-afternoon, were on our way toward Daliat el Carmel, near Haifa, where we were to meet our Druze sheik, Adel Mefleh Halaby. It was unbelievably quiet when we arrived in Daliat. The Moslems were either praying or preparing to do so; the Jews were either preparing for the Saturday Sabbath or hanging out with friends in coffee shops.

We located Mr Halaby's restaurant and souvenir shop, and, after one of his grandchildren went to see where he was, we were invited to his house, a large concrete structure a short distance away from the business district. After a delightful afternoon with this fascinating subject, we drove the hour-long trip to Tel Aviv, extremely fatigued but ecstatically happy with the results of the last few frantic days.

MAY 7-10:   Saturday night, May 7, was a "show and tell" party in our Tel Aviv apartment. A group of friends and relatives came to dinner, then urged us to show the paintings and videotapes we had made thus far. Lunda was thrilled by their enthusiastic reactions to her work, while I was gratified to evoke a few laughs when I related some of our misadventures, especially the frantic two days we spent in Safed and atop Mount Meron.

On Sunday, May 8, we finally were able to paint and interview the urban Bedouin woman, Nama, and her daughter, Abir. Ultimately, I decided not to use them in the book. Perhaps they will appear in a sequel.

Monday morning, May 9, we went to visit Achsa Lapid, a cousin of Ruth's who is an internationally-acclaimed expert in the art of quilting. She also makes an unusual line of clothing. We were quite impressed with her talent and both Lunda and I now have samples of her work. Although Lunda painted her and I took innumerable photographs, this subject, as was the urban Bedouin, is being held for possible inclusion in a sequel.

Since we had been invited to attend an authentic henna ceremony that evening, we left Achsa's house early enough to witness this colorful ritual from start to finish. These elaborate ceremonies can go on and on interminably. We loved it, but by the time we left it was midnight – and still going on!

Tuesday, May 10, was spent at home in Tel Aviv, preparing for the next day's journey to the Negev Desert to meet with the desert Bedouin.

MAY 11: Once again, Elisha and Dantchu arranged to meet "somewhere along the road", and as desolate as that road turned out to be, sure enough, Dantchu somehow managed to meet us. For this trip, Dantchu drove his own car. This was because he would be staying over that night to give a slide show and historical lecture to Israeli troops stationed in the area. Later I was to learn that Dantchu was considered an expert on the history and geography of the Holy Land. I guess that explains his uncanny knack of meeting us way out in the middle of nowhere. He is a most interesting traveling companion, and, whenever he rode with us, he was like a tour guide, relating a non-stop history of the places and people we were going to visit. Just a little aside here – Dantchu taught himself English by reading, so never had the benefit of hearing the correct pronunciation of some words. I taped every word he said along the trips and when I listened to the tapes afterwards, there were some words I just could not figure out. As an example, while relating Jewish history he kept using the word "babillions". It took me a while to figure out that he meant "Babylonians".

Dantchu's friend, Sefi Hanegbi, had made the arrangements for our meeting with the desert Bedouin. I seriously doubt that we could have met with these shy, traditional people without his intercession. Sefi is quite a story in himself. He is a camel trader, who, through the years, has done a considerable amount of business with the Bedouin. He uses the camels for his "Million Star Hotel" business called Camel Riders, which sells desert safaris to tourists. Traveling on camelback and camping under the stars seems to be quite popular, and my idea of a fun thing to do. This may surprise you, but reservations are definitely a requirement.

Our visit with the Bedouin family was probably the most enjoyable time I had during the entire trip. It was so different from anything I had ever witnessed before. There was such a simple charm about the Bedouin, a warmth and sweetness of spirit that was captivating.

After saying goodbye to our Bedouin friends, who were fasting for the Moslem period of Ramadan, we stopped for a picnic lunch. Sefi related some charming Bedouin stories which I included in that chapter, then left us to return to the desert. The rest of us motored to a nearby area called Mitzpai Rimon, known for its natural and magnificent crater.

We pulled into a roadside stop for soft drinks and Elisha struck up a conversation with the owner. They were discussing the man who owned the gas station in the area and an incident concerning our eldest son, who stopped at this very spot for gas about a month earlier. I must interject here that our four children all bear a strong resemblance to Elisha, especially our eldest, Harel. When Harel returned home from that trip, he told us a story that was hard to believe. It seems that, while servicing Harel's car, the owner kept staring at him. When our son presented his credit card, the man saw the name Cohen and excitedly asked if he was the son of Elisha Cohen. It turned out that this man had served under Elisha in the War of Independence more than forty years ago. They had not seen each other since, but Elisha had saved the man's life at great risk of his own. Since Elisha never talks about his military career, none of the family knew of his heroics until Harel heard the story from the man at the gas station.

Elisha excused himself and walked with the restaurant owner to the gas station. He returned with a third man about ten minutes later; it was the station owner, who was so emotional about meeting Elisha again that he just stood there, hugging and kissing his hero. Well, Lunda and I were close to tears, as was Elisha, although he would never admit to such sentimentality.

At the insistence of Elisha's friend, we went to the man's home, where the two men reminisced about their army days, while Lunda and I seized the opportunity to use the bathroom facilities, "showering" in the basin to rid ourselves of the desert sand.

It was getting dark, and I was becoming nervous about driving through the desert at night. Normally, I would not have worried, but, before this trip, I had noticed that Elisha had packed his gun (a fact I do not believe Lunda realized). By the time we left, the sun was setting, and if I had had a tranquilizer I would have taken it at that moment. I know now that I should have left the navigating to Elisha, but when I saw a sign which read "Gaza 17 kilometres" I panicked. Talking to Elisha in agitated Hebrew so as not to alarm Lunda, I insisted that we were on the wrong road. My overactive imagination could picture Arab snipers lying in ambush ahead. Of course, had I been the least bit rational at the time, I would have realized that the Israeli border patrol would have stopped us before we entered Gaza. To calm my fears, Elisha turned the car around and drove all the way back to the last village we had passed to verify directions. He was assured that he had taken the right road, and that, if he had continued on it a bit farther, he would have seen the turn-off to Tel Aviv. Needless to say, I kept my mouth shut the rest of the way home, opening it only to gulp down a hefty scotch with Lunda when we got there.

Even the hold-outs of the tribe have fallen prey to Western influence. The desert Bedouin are avid followers of "Dynasty"!

MAY 14:   We went to the town of Ramla for the Yemenite groom's Sabbath. A week earlier, this couple had been married, and it is traditional for the following Sabbath to be hosted by the groom's family. Since we had missed the wedding, we did not want to insult the family by not showing up for this occasion.

We spent part of the day with the family and their friends, praying and eating, and eating, and eating. The Yemenite food they served was delicious if a bit spicy. Poor Lunda, who had experienced several misadventures with food in China and Africa, could not get anything past her lips. The food was not the hottest aspect of this day, but rather the really torrid temperature – over a hundred degrees – and the lack of air-conditioning. By early afternoon we were soaking wet, totally exhausted and somewhat nauseous. Finally, having stayed long enough to fulfill our social obligation, we said our goodbyes and left, not without some objections. Thank God the car was air-conditioned, allowing us to revive somewhat on the long ride home.

MAY 15:   This Sunday turned out to be the hottest day of the year. We were in the midst of a heatwave, but we were also on a tight schedule which we had to keep. We had to collect one of the Yemenite groom's sisters, then drive to the house of the "dresser" in a remote town called Ekron, where the temperature soared to 120 degrees! Ilana Said, our Yemenite bride, sat down and, with nothing more than a small electric fan to cool her, subjected herself to two hours of being decked out in the unbelievably heavy bridal raiment you saw in her portrait. Amazingly, she smiled and laughed through the whole ordeal and even expressed her gratitude to us for having chosen her as a subject. When we finally were finished with the painting and interviewing, we took Ilana home, then drove back to Tel Aviv for a cool, quiet and, fortunately, uneventful evening.

MAY 16:   The heatwave continues! But Ruth Dayan has kindly agreed to come to my house to sit for Lunda. For such a celebrated personage, Ruth is terribly camera-shy. She asked me not to videotape her, but I sneaked a few shots of her to include in my personal "highlights" cassette.

MAY 17:   I spent most of the day researching the Ethiopians in the archives of the Museum of the Diaspora (in Tel Aviv). By sheer coincidence, the museum was presenting an Ethiopian exhibition this week and had even constructed a reproduction of a typical Ethiopian house (a circular, straw-roofed structure). They also had chronicled the events of their lives in Ethiopia, the several dramatic airlifts to Israel, their absorption into the fabric of Israeli society and their current grievances.

MAY 18:   We drove to Jerusalem, where, after spending the morning on a walking tour of the Old City, we went to the residence of the Syrian Orthodox Archbishop, Dionysius Behnam Jajjawi. He wanted to show us his historic old church, but it was decided by Elisha that we should leave the Old City before sundown, so we politely declined the invitation, promising to return at some future date.

As we left Jerusalem, we reviewed what we had done in a relatively short period of time.

MAY 19-23:   We interspersed our packing with visiting family and friends. On the 19th, we were invited by Ruth to attend a Circassian wedding and accepted with alacrity. It was a gay and beautiful occasion and gave us an emotional lift that sustained us for the remaining few days of our stay.

Lunda left for her home in California to do the final paintings. A few days later, Elisha and I returned to our home in New Jersey, where my research and writing work would really begin.

SELECT BIBLIOGRAPHY

Aescoly, A.Z. 1973. *Sefer Haralashim*. 2nd ed. Jerusalem: Reuben Mass Press.

Alexandrov, Victor. 1967. *The Kremlin, Nerve Center of Russia*. Leicester: Blackfriars Press.

Ausubel, Nathan. 1964. *The Book of Jewish Knowledge*. New York: Crown Publishers.

Ben-Zvi, Itzhak. 1957. *The Exiled and the Redeemed*. Trans. Isaac A. Abbady, Philadelphia.

Braslavsky, Joseph. 1954. *Research of Our Country*. Israel: Kibbutz Hameuchad, Publishers.

Brown, J.R. 1963. *Temple and Sacrifice in Rabbinic Judaism*. The Winslow Lectures, Seabury-Western Theological Seminary, Evanston, Illinois.

Cazin, Paul. 1961. *Poland*. France: Hatchette World Albums.

Chatty, Dawn. 1985. *From Camel to Truck: The Bedouin in the Modern World*. New York: Vantage Press.

Crooke, William. 1921. *Herklot's Islam in India*. London: Humphrey Milford, Oxford University Press.

Devi, Pria, and R. Kurin. *Aditi, the Living Arts of India*. Washington, DC: Smithsonian Institute Press.

Dobrinsky, Herbert C. 1980. *Selected Laws and Customs of Shepardic Jewry*. New York: Yeshiva University.

Encyclopaedia Brittanica, 1971 edition, s.v. "Trade."

Encyclopaedia Brittanica, 1971 edition, s.v. "Hinna."

Falah, Ghazi. *The Role of the British Administration in the Sedenterization of the Bedouin Tribes in Northern Palestine 1918-1948*. North Carolina: Center for Middle Eastern and Islamic Studies, University of Durham

Frumkin, Jacob, Gregor Aronson, Goldweiser and Joseph Lewitan (eds). 1969. *Russian Jewry 1917-1967*. A.S. Barnes & Co.

Gersh, Harry. 1964. *The Story of the Jew*. Revised ed. New York: Berman House.

Goiten, S.D. 1964. *Jews and Arabs, Their Contacts through the Ages*. New York: Schocken Books.

Grelot, Pierre. 1964. *Man and Wife in Scripture*. New York: Herder and Herder.

Haddad, H. 1984. *Jews of Arab and Islamic Countries*. New York: Shengold.

1974 Hassan Ali, Meer. 1974. *Observations of the Mussalmauns of India*. London: Humphrey Milford, Oxford University Press.

Henderson, Peter. 1890. *Henderson's Handbook of Plants and General Horticulture*. New York: Peter Henderson and Co.

The Jewish Encyclopedia, 1902 edition, s.v. "Atonement."

Johnson, Paul. 1988. *A History of the Jews*. New York: Harper & Row.

Kaufman, Shelemay Kay. 1986. *Music, Ritual and Falasha History*. East Lansig: Michigan State University, African Studies Center.

—— (ed.). 1986. *The Jews of Ethiopia, a People in Transition*. Guest Curator Nahum Goldman Museum of the Jewish Diaspora, Tel Aviv and the Jewish Museum, New York.

Kessler, David. 1982. *The Falashas: The Forgotten Jews of Ethiopia*. London: George Allen & Unwin.

Kolatch, Alfred J. 1981. *The Jewish Book of Why*. New York: Jonathan David Publishers.

Leslau, Wolf. 1951. *Falasha Anthology*. New Haven, Connecticut.

Levinger, Ehrlich, Rabbi J. Lee and wife Elma. 1928. *The Story of the Jew*.

Marx, Emanuel, and Avshalom Shmueli (eds). 1984. *The Changing Bedouin*. New Brunswick, Connecticut: Transaction Books.

McDowell, Bart. 1977. *Journey Across Russia, the Soviet Union Today*. National Geographic Society.

Meinertzhagen, Col. Richard. 1959. *Middle East Diary 1917-1956*. New York: Thomas Yoseloff.

Moran, Lord. 1966. *Churchill, Taken from the Diaries of Lord Moran*. Boston: Houghton Mifflin.

Parfitt, Tudor. 1985. *Operation Moses*. London: Weidenfeld & Nicolson.

Pearlman, Moshe. 1973. *In the*

Footsteps of Moses. Israel: Steimatzky's Agency and Nateev Publishing.

——. 1975. *In the Footsteps of the Prophets*. New York: Thomas Y. Crowell Co.

Quirin, James. 1977. 'The Beta Israel (Falasha)', in Ethiopian History. Caste Formation and Culture Change 1270-1868. PhD dissertation. University of Minnesota.

Rappoport, Louis. 1986. *The Story of Operation Moses*. New York: Harcourt, Brace, Jovanovich.

Ronart, Stephan and Nandy. 1960. *Concise Encyclopedia of Arabic Civilization*. New York: Frederick A. Praeger, Inc.

Seltzer, Leon S. (ed.). 1952. *The Columbia Lippincott Gazetteer*. New York: Columbia University Press. s.v. "Circassions."

Ullendorf, Edward. 1965. *The Ethiopians*. London: Oxford University Press.

——. 1968. *Ethiopia and the Bible*. London: Oxford University Press.

Vishniac, Roman. 1965. *Polish Jews, A Pictorial Record*. New York: Schocken Books.

Weir, Shelagh. 1989. *Palestinian Costume*. Austin: University of Texas Press.

Wiesel, Eli. 1966. *The Jews of Silence*. Canada: Holt, Rinehart, Weinstein.

Yadin, Yigael. 1971. *Bar Kokhba*. New York: Random House.